THE SHAMAN'S
Path

THE SHAMAN'S
Path

A Guided Journey to Discover Your Healed Self

LORIE ALLEN

authorHOUSE®

AuthorHouse™
1663 Liberty Drive
Bloomington, IN 47403
www.authorhouse.com
Phone: 1-800-839-8640

Published by AuthorHouse   05/09/2013

ISBN: 978-1-4817-3965-8 (sc)
ISBN: 978-1-4817-3964-1 (hc)
ISBN: 978-1-4817-3963-4 (e)

Library of Congress Control Number: 2013906721

To Howard W. Allen, with all my love

for my parents, without whose love and support this work would not have been possible;

and, for Zoe Elizabeth, who taught me how to journey

CONTENTS

PART TWO
TOOLS FOR HEALING

APPENDICES

ACKNOWLEDGEMENTS

Many have helped me as this project evolved. My husband, who always knew I was more than a tad off the mainstream, has been validated in his belief by this new path of mine, but he has always offered support and strength. My colleague and friend, Peggy Galantowicz, read the manuscript several times in the beginning, turning her eye to clarity and continuity. Michele Mekel offered her enthusiasm and knowledge, and editorial expertise that tied the work into a sensible whole. Her Eagle-eyed review of the final project made it feel, to me, like a real book. Judith Bush encouraged me to write songs in English. Zoe Elizabeth Allen showed me how to dive into the Lower World, and sent me vivid mental pictures of fascinating places to visit. I cannot thank them all enough.

Mine has been a journey of transformation and joy. My wish is that you also find some level of enlightenment and healing as you step upon this path.

Lorie Allen, Carbondale, IL 2013

Using This Book

This project began as an attempt to type up my workshop notes so they would be legible if ever I wanted to re-read them. As I went to workshops, and added and rearranged what was being presented, and as my experience and understanding increased, my notes took on a life of their own. My notebook was expanding. The words were no longer the words of an individual teacher or presenter or those quoted from one of the various books I found to devour on this subject. As I began to practice what I learned in classes, the words shaped themselves into a framework that made more sense to me for the 21st century.

I found that other students in my group had different experiences. In many cases, their instructions differed from those I heard and wrote in my journal. In an oral tradition, when given instructions, you are limited to what you write down or what you remember. For me, this was a small problem. For a while, I was quite unsure of what to do, how to do it, or even if this was something I should practice. Then a friend suggested I write a workbook, which could be used in classes, so all the instructions, at least, would be clear and consistent. So, this project continued with the intent of helping to move the traditional teachings from the oral tradition to the written.

Then, one day I took a journey to the Upper World. There, I met an extraordinary being. He explained to me that the ways of the Shamans of the high Andes are good ways to connect with the

Earth, and the spirits of the land, the waters, and the mountains. People outside of Peru need to learn these ways, but they should be adapted to their own land. I felt there needed to be a way for people to learn to practice the essence of this teaching outside of Peru, without needing to incur either the expense of taking a week-long residential training course, or traveling to Peru. The Quechuan language has lovely nuances understood by the Apus, the mountain spirits, of Peru. In North America, English or Spanish or French are the languages most used. In order to help as many people as possible get in touch with the Earth, it was time for the oral traditions to be written, and to evolve in a new way, on new continents. I have attempted to begin that process.

The exercises in this book are designed as a process and work best when completed over the course of one to three years. Done in the order of shedding self, shedding past, recognizing your destiny, and then walking in the collective, a cycle around the directions from South to West to North to East is completed. The journey I completed was directed under the guidance of talented Shamanic teachers who have journeyed often in Peru and are working to preserve the original traditions. They, and other talented and dedicated individuals from around the globe, do this through a series of small group classes that are usually filled by word of mouth.

Several exercises, with complete instructions for doing the work on your own, or with other people, are included in each chapter. Over the course of the exercises, you will collect 13 stones and one beautiful 22" x 24" cloth to hold them. You will also need a bottle of Florida Water and a pendulum. More information about those items is included in Chapter One. Stones you need will be listed at the beginning of each chapter. Most other supplies you need will be found in nature, your local bookstore, craft shop, grocery store, flower shop, or on-line. This work is very personal, and what you choose to use is up to you. Before you begin to find stones to include in the work, read in depth about your Mesa in Chapter Seven, Care and Feeding of Your Mesa and Power Animals.

You may choose to do this work on your own. You may choose to find a group of friends and take this trip together. Whichever way you are able to start transforming on this path, begin now. The Shamans have said that the Earth needs to wake up now. They have come down from the mountains to share this work and especially to share it with the people of North America and Europe. And, they want it shared quickly. Small classes, taught by a few people, are not getting the word out fast enough. The language is a barrier, as well. My hope is, that by reading this book, you will practice some of the exercises and begin to wake up your land. I also hope that you will gather like-minded friends and begin to do this work regularly as a group. Perhaps, you will find a class and have the added wisdom of an experienced Shaman to guide you. In the collective, in the Ayllu, you are able to create, comes a shared purpose and faster transformation.

Most important, at this point in time, is sacred ceremony. Light a fire. Create Despachos for your land. They need not be elaborate, just a gift from your heart to your land. Walk in right relationship, in Ayni, with those beings around you. Walk with all beings, the Standing Talls, the Plant People, the Stone People, the Finned, the

Furred, and the Creepy Crawlies. Each has something to teach us about ourselves and about our world. In this way, the work of the Shamans of the high Andes will be continued and expanded. Their sacrifices will not be in vain. The Earth will wake from her long slumber and hold us sweetly as we sing. Then, in this dance of life, we shall be thrice blessed.

INTRODUCTION

This book was developed as an aid to those seeking a new way of being in the world. The workshops I completed were based on a combination of a traditional Native American Medicine Wheel and the practice and philosophy of the Andean Shamans. These teachings have been supplemented with information about chakra healing, using a pendulum to measure an energy field, and my life experiences as a healer in both Healing Touch and Reiki. By completing the exercises in this book, you will create a Healer's Mesa, grounded in the cosmology of the Shamans of the high Andes of Peru, and adapted for personal use in North America and elsewhere.

Traditionally, this has been an oral tradition. Handed down from one teacher to another over the course of centuries, the knowledge expands and is modified as it moves by word of mouth across time and space. What is presented here is both old and new. Some of the techniques have been revised to be accessible to individuals or small groups working together without a Shamanic teacher. Songs are presented in Quechuan and in English (if a translation was available), and some have been musically annotated so that anyone who reads music can learn to sing them. If you do not sing, speak the words in a rhythmic way. The whole is designed to flow, to encircle, and to embrace its followers on a path of personal healing and enlightenment.

This energetic way of healing oneself and others is an
experiential exploration into the nature of time, energy, and
the true self, as well as a personal journey into empowerment
and spiritual growth. The program includes the four directions
honored by indigenous peoples around the world since the Ancient
Ones walked the Earth. And, although this book focuses on an
Incan/Peruvian Shamanic tradition and cosmology, it has been
adapted for individual and small group use in North America and
elsewhere. The cosmology of the high Andes is just now coming
to the West, and those studying the ways of the Pampamesayoq
and Altomesayoq Shamans of Peru are working to preserve the
heart of this program, which has been practiced in a similar way
for thousands of years. Hidden from the Spanish, many of the
ceremonies blended with Catholicism, and their teaching now is
not so much a "religion" as a way of being in nature.

The work of this program strengthens your connection to
nature and enables you to understand the Shaman's way of seeing.
You will learn valuable tools for healing through working with
your own stones and connecting to the lineage of the medicine
people of the high Andes and to Mother Earth, Pachamama.
Some of this work can be done alone. Other parts are best done
with others. Sometimes, after a weekend retreat, the teacher
will offer rites of passage. These rites honor the nature of the
program, and recognize the personal growth experienced, as one
becomes a Wisdom Keeper, a Caretaker of the Earth. You may
be given a lineage stone, usually from Peru, as a gift from your
Shaman-teacher. However, this work is deeply personal, and much
can be done on your own. If you wish to deepen your connection

with your own land and with nature, and to better understand yourself, then this work may speak to you.

When taking a workshop, the program is completed over the course of four long weekends over two full years. This allows plenty of time for integration of the cosmology into your own version of reality, as well as opportunity to practice and implement what you are learning. I recommend that you take your time when moving through the exercises for that reason. The work can also be done over the period of a year or two on your own. Looking at the program in its traditional format, the first fourth works with energy of the South, and you learn the Serpent Way, Amaru. This is a path of personal healing through which you shed the past as the serpent sheds its skin. You begin to transform your wounds into sources of power and compassion. Here, in the work of the South, you learn to bring "the flow" back into your life. The work links you to a lineage of medicine women and men of the high Andes. Your stones are transformed, and the Mesa created by you becomes that of a Healer.

In the second session, you step into the Jaguar Way of the West, Chocochinchi. There, you step beyond fear and violence, and go into the void where transformation lives and can occur. You learn about your own connections to power. Here the work connects you to, and transform you into, a Caretaker of the Earth.

In the North, the Hummingbird, or Kenti, Way, you learn the way of the ancestors, the Ancient Ones. The lessons here are the practice of invisibility and stepping out of time. You practice stillness in motion and earn the Wisdom Keeper rites.

The final session provides rites that reconnect you to the stars. The Eagle/Condor Way of the East, Apuchin, is the way of the visionary. You learn to embrace your true nature and to take your gifts out into the world. Here you learn to access how to walk in the world from your healed state and to call in your fulfilled state. You become ready to "dream the world into being."

As you practice the exercises in this book and learn to journey, you join many others on a path of healing and restoration. It is prophesized that, as we heal and restore ourselves, the wheel mends and becomes a rainbow of peace. It is my wish that your practice of the ceremonies available to all of us for personal growth and transformation leads you to a path of self-growth and learning where we can all dream the world into a state of peace.

PART ONE
THE SHAMAN'S PATH

ONE

Exploring the Nature of Time, Energy, and Your True Self

The cosmology of the Shamans of the high Andes works with several overlying archetypes and ways of being that are easily adapted to the traditional North American Medicine Wheel. The work also involves ceremony. Gifts to the Earth are prepared, blessed, and given to sacred fire, where they are consumed by the various spirit energies of the land. The following definitions and explanation of terms are adapted from information given orally by my teachers and guides, and modified as my experience with the work has increased.

As you do the work outlined in the following pages, you will be opening Sacred Space, creating gifts for your land, and creating fire ceremonies. Instructions for doing these steps are presented here first and often more deeply explained later. As you progress in your healing and as your understanding of ceremony grows, your ability to create your own ceremonies and to trust your intuition expands.

Throughout the chapters are exercises for you to complete to enhance your healing and spiritual growth. Some exercises you can complete on your own. In others, you will need a partner. You will learn to travel with the Shamanic journey. My personal experiences are included as an example of what you might expect. Every person's path is different. We are all colored by our past experiences. My goal in presenting this material is to provide guidance for spiritual growth, as well as to offer a concrete method of actually "doing something" to help your land specifically, and Mother Earth, generally.

The Earth needs stewardship now more than at any other time in her life's story. Those who do this work are able to offer that healing and guidance in a very powerful way. Bright blessings to you as you begin this journey. Let the adventure of transformation begin!

The Archetypes

This journey follows a path based on Peruvian mythology and spirituality that is now being adapted for study in North America and Europe. Many terms are in the Quechuan language, which is just now being put into a written form. Many of these terms are easily translated into American English. Many of them hold more than just a translation, as the vibration of the words also carry meaning. The journey begins with an exploration of the foundation of the cosmology, as well as some of the early legends and stories. Most of those legends and stories speak to us in symbols and, like our dreams, are sometimes difficult to interpret. Archetypal symbols that speak to most people at different levels are key.

In the South is Serpent, also called Sachamama, or Amaru, the Mother of the Waters. This is the archetype of the healer throughout many cultures. She teaches us to shed our personal past the way she sheds her skin. This is the primary life force of the one who dives deep and who knows the way into the deepest places inside of ourselves, as well as the Hujupacha, the Lower World, the realm of the unconscious. Amaru, moving with beauty on the belly of the Mother, knows the way back to the original Garden of Eden, the place of innocence.

In the West is Jaguar, also called Otorongo, or Chocochinchi, Mother-Sister Jaguar knows the way across the Rainbow Bridge that connects us to the world of mystery. In the Middle World, the Kaypacha, she is the one who swallows the dying sun, teaching us to step beyond fear, violence, and death. Her archetypal connection is to the life force of the jungle, everything that is green. She is the steward of the life force. She is the "Luminous Warrior" who has no enemies in this world or the next, and she represents the principles of life, death, and renewal.

In the North is Hummingbird, Kenti, and the place of the ancestors, grandmothers and grandfathers, ancient memories, and ancient wisdom. Those who have stepped outside of time can slip through the veil to help us remember the ancient ways. These are the ways of Kenti, Hummingbird, who drinks directly from the nectar of life. Although not built for flight, Hummingbird undertakes and accomplishes the impossible journey.

Condor/Eagle, Apuchin, is the great archetype of the East, the place of the rising Sun, the place of our Be-coming and embraces the principle of seeing from a high perspective, with a vision of clarity and beauty. The great wings of the Condor hold the heart and teach us to see with the eyes of the heart. Here, we are pushed out of the nest to spread our own wings so that we may always fly wing to wing with the Great Spirit. With Apuchin, we can travel to the Upper World, the Hanaqpacha.

In addition to the three worlds and concepts of flow, connectivity, and framework, there are other beings to encounter on the path and common terms that need to be defined. The most important of these is Huascar, the Lord of Life and the Lord of Death. Historically, Huascar was one of two sons of Pacha Kuti Inka (the Inka who read the prophecy of bearded men with sticks that spoke with fire who would turn the world upside down). Huascar was the keeper of the medicine teachings of the Inka. His brother, who helped the Spanish to conquer his people, killed him. Huascar was not able to complete his Ayni (right relationship, balance, reciprocity) before his death. Therefore, he went to the Lower World, Hujupacha, and became the harmonizing agent there. The Lower World is a chaotic, dark place full of all creative potential. Huascar is the renewer of the Earth, and represents our own personal need of renewing our own Earth, our own fallow fields, and places that need aerating. The gift of Huascar is to harmonize our relationship with our Shadow. When you journey to the Lower World, you ask Huascar's permission to enter, and he often will help you on your travels.

Quetzalcoatl is the Lord of the Morning/the Dawn, the Day Bringer, and the Morning Star. As an archetype, he is shared by other traditions and known by other names: Kokopelli, Kukulkan, and Koni Raya. Quetzal is a beautiful jungle bird. Coatl is a serpent, a reptile. Together, they form a feathered, winged serpent that has acquired flight. As such, he is the organizer of the Middle World, Kaypacha, who brought irrigation, medicine plants, and stonework, and, walking in the Americas, brought stability, music, dance, flutes, and drums. Although awareness of this archetype has been lost in much of North American culture, we can call on it individually as an animistic knowledge of the ways of the Earth. Quetzalcoatl organizes your relationship with the Middle World. When you come into right relationship with Quetzalcoatl, you do not have to micromanage your life.

Pacha Kuti was an Inkan king, father of Huascar, who was given the prophecy that the world was turning over with the coming of the Spanish. He is the keeper of the possibilities and is the organizing agent of the Hanaqpacha, the Upper World. Developing a connection to the Hanaqpacha, with its concept of circular time, offers the possibility of stepping outside of linear time, thereby making time stand still. Coming into relationship with Pacha Kuti brings heavenly order, allows us to recognize what can be changed, and helps us to change it before it is born.

You need to develop your own relationship with these archetypes. As you work with them as you journey in their worlds, your descriptions will grow and come from your own experience.

Despacho

A Despacho is a gift to the spirits of the land. Created in a ceremony of meditation and prayer, the gift honors Mother Earth, the waters of the Earth, Father Sky, the Star Nations, and the mountain spirits of Peru and elsewhere. A Despacho ceremony is a central ceremony of exchange and is often celebrated for the purpose of bringing situations into Ayni, into balance, right relationship, and harmony.

The Despacho ceremony is a gift of love and communion. It is an "envelope" filled with gifts and prayers offered through our sacred breath. Each item offers a prayer and gift of power that sparks the momentum for energy shifts. It brings an individual, a couple, or a group into harmonious relationship with all that is.

A Despacho encompasses the balance of yachi (right thinking), of munay (right loving), and of yanqui (right doing). It includes the three worlds of the Hujupacha (the Lower World), the Kaypacha (the Middle World), and the Hanaqpacha (the Upper World). It honors the organizing principles of Amaru (fluidity), Chocochinchi (connectivity), and Apuchin (framework).

Despachos are used for balancing, gratitude, healing, shifting, honoring, and transitions. They can be used, with intent, to bring things, like relationships, homes, businesses, and health, into right relationship. This lovely gift is most often burned in a fire ceremony, but it may also be buried. Some can be created so they can be immersed in water or tossed gently into a lake or stream. Traditionally, Despachos are burned at either high noon or at dusk when there are no shadows. The spirits of the land do not wish to be seen by their shadow when accepting your gift. When you place your Despacho in the fire, turn your back and wait a few minutes to allow the spirits to enter the Sacred Space to receive your offering. Then, keeping your back turned, slowly walk away from the fire. The spirits of the land are honored by the gift and wish to consume it privately. Return the next morning to see what is left. Sometimes part of the gift remains and should be buried. At other times, what is left is a gift from the spirits of the land to you. You will instinctively know which is a gift to you or which is to be buried. At a recent fire, a single red carnation remained the next morning. Only slightly singed by the fire that consumed everything else, it was clear this was a gift to the Ayllu who created the Despacho.

Fire Ceremony

The transformational fire ceremony is done on the full moon of each month and other times of the year as the need arises. Traditionally, one participated in fire ceremonies for approximately a three-year period before beginning to do them for one's self. Then another three-year period was spent doing them alone (or with your teacher) before attempting to do one for others. Until recently, this was the training process for this ceremony. Now, Shamans say that there is "no time" for this lengthy process. The Earth and our civilization are in such great peril that students should begin to do the fire ceremony as soon as they are guided to do so. In my experience, the fire then becomes the teacher. It will let you know immediately if your intention or attitude is not pure or in tune with the tradition.

One should always begin the ceremony by establishing Sacred Space. After lighting the fire, a chant is begun to call upon the spirits of the waters beneath the Earth and bring them in harmony with the land. This chant makes the fire "friendly." In essence:

O Great Mother, Mother of the Waters;
We call on you, waters of our birth.
Waters of our sustenance;
Waters that cleanse us on our death; waters of life.

Then, a song to call on the Apus of Peru and the spirits of your land is added. Other places, such as local lakes, rivers, or mountains, can be added as you are called upon to do so. The chanting continues until the fire becomes "friendly" and is burning well without too much smoke.

Olive oil and essential sweet oils such as lavender, rose, or musk, can be used as offerings during the taming of the fire. The moment the fire becomes friendly, it changes color and burns in a different manner. This change should be learned from direct observation and experience with the fire. You discover the friendly fire yourself. Trust that you will instinctively recognize when the fire is just right. Kneel at the fire and offer your prayers to the item you are giving. Toss the item(s) into the fire with prayer and with the intent that your prayers will be answered. There is no need to turn your back or walk away when making an offering to the fire. Only when offering the Despacho, do the spirits of the land require privacy.

View this information as the "heart" of the ceremony. The style of your teacher does not need to be literally copied; it is just a beginning point from which you find your own ritual to add to the ceremony. What follows is one method to prepare for your first fire ceremony. In some ceremonies, one gives up the old <u>and</u> invites in the new in the act of coming to the fire. Others create Ayni (right relationship or balance) or honor the dead. Ceremonies may be created for almost any purpose you intend: a new job; a marriage; a move; a birth; a death; joy in the day. The ceremonies may be as creative and different as their purpose, or they may follow a set formula.

There are two main types of fire ceremony. One is a fire of purification, and the other is a fire of transformation. The ones done in this cosmology are fires of transformation. Ceremonies can (and, perhaps, should) be done once a month on the full moon. Or they can be done at the new moon, depending on your purpose. Or they can be done anytime you are called on to offer prayers to the Earth and your land. Ceremonies can be done either at noon or at dusk, when there is no shadow. Anytime anything is troubling you, do ceremony. In other words, there are no rules so long as your intent is pure.

For the first fire ceremony, define several of your issues, both positive and negative. For example, write down three aspects of spirit or character that you would like to invite into your life or have more powerfully expressed in your life, such as courage, creativity, focus, etc. Next, write down three aspects that you would like to have healed, such as confusion, cowardice, complaining, etc. With focused intent, blow your prayers, desires, and dreams onto the papers you have written and place them in the fire. Let the negative issues go with your prayers into the fire. Using your hands to move the smoke around you, bring the positive issues into your body with the smoke.

After your first fire ceremony, the process of preparation is simpler. For later fire ceremonies, you choose one important healing issue, either something you want to invite in or something you want to let go, and create an offering, a light arrow that represents this out of materials that are burnable. Offerings can be as simple as a small stick decorated with red or white ribbon or a flower, herbs, tobacco, or incense. Or you might create a Despacho. These need not be an art project, although the gifts are often beautiful. These gifts are a way to focus your attention in an active meditation. There are only two warnings concerning the fire ceremony: (1) your wish cannot involve personal material gain, and (2) your wish may not manipulate another person's will.

During the ceremony, you chant and wait for the fire to become "friendly." Put another way, you wait until you come up to the temperature of the fire. No, you do not become hotter and turn red. But, you will notice that your body begins to tingle and may vibrate a little. You transform to the vibration of the fire. You may not experience this sensation during your first fires. Make your offering when it feels right for you to do so. You cannot do this wrong. Whenever you approach the fire with your gift, it is the right time. Then approach the fire and silently put your offering or a gift of tobacco or incense into it. Next, move your hands through the smoke. Draw the energy of the fire into your belly, your heart, and your forehead. Then allow the smoke to move over your energy body, pulling the smoke around you with your hands. This helps you to focus your attention and energy upon your own transformation. When offering a Despacho, place the Despacho in the fire last, turning your back to the fire as the spirits of the land come to receive your gift. Go back the next morning (or several hours later to be sure the fire is burned down and safe for the night), and bury any items that may be left.

There is a two-week period following a fire ceremony in which "instances of opportunity" appear. These "instances" provide the "opportunity" to translate your intent for healing into reality. You are advised to think of the fire ceremony, not as an instantaneous magical change, but rather as an opening for healing distinctive habits and patterns. Recognize this "opening," and seize the opportunity to change your behavior in the real world. Then let the Universe take care of the details.

Ritual Clearing

There are many ways of ritually cleansing or "clearing" your stones, your body, and your home. Quite a few good books have been written on this topic and are listed in the bibliography. Sage, cedar, or other incense waved over people or objects or wafted into corners is a common way to clear yourself and your home of stuck or unwanted energy. Stones are often buried, washed in salt water, or set in the sun or moonlight to cleanse. Card sets, used for predicting the future or helping to answer questions, are cleared with smoke, as well as by holding each card to your heart center with the intention of removing the energy of others who might have touched your deck.

In this cosmology, however, there is only one way to clear anything, and that is by spritzing Florida Water. Take a small sip and spit. The Florida Water sprays into space or over the object to be cleared. Each time you use your Mesa stones, clear them. Before you close your Mesa, clear it. When you open Sacred Space, a little spray of Florida Water honors each of the directions. Using a tarot deck with friends? Clear it. Acquire some beautiful new stones? Clear them. One spritz usually works fine. No, you may not use a little spray bottle. Over time, you will learn to create a fine spray without dribbling too much down your chin or swallowing too much.

Florida Water is a 19th-century formula for a commercially prepared toilet water that blends an array of floral essential oils in a water-alcohol base. The name refers to the fabled Fountain of Youth said to have been located in Florida. Florida Water has been widely used in rituals of home protection and spiritual cleansing since the 19th - century. There are many blends and recipes available. Because of the alcohol content, none of them "taste" very good. Over time, you get used to the burn as you open Sacred Space and spit. Florida Water is readily available on Ebay.com and via other sources, as well as at Mexican groceries, and it is not expensive. There are recipes on-line for making your own, generally a gallon at a time. One good site, as of this writing, is http://hoodoo-conjure.com/formulas/florida-water.html. However, I have been doing this work for several years and just started to use my third bottle. It lasts so long that making my own has never made sense (and, judging by the ingredients I've seen, it would not taste better either).

Opening Sacred Space

In this cosmology, space is opened first in the South. Next, the West is welcomed, followed by the North. After greeting the spirits of the East, Pachamama, the Earth Mother is greeted. Last are Father Sky, Grandmother Moon and the Star Nations. A prayer of welcome is said in each direction. Often, specific prayers for the work being done or the intention of the ceremony is added. Indeed, once you get the general idea of opening Sacred Space, you will probably make up your own prayer each time you do ceremony.

To begin, stand facing the direction you wish to welcome. Hold your left hand up toward that direction while your right hand rattles. Use your bottle of Florida Water to create a whistle to call the spirits. Then state your invocation or prayer. Spray a small sip of Florida Water to that direction. Continue to rattle, whistle, pray, and spit in each direction. This offers energy, prayers, and cleansing to each of the directions.

In this work, you will open space each time you go to a Nature Painting, start a fire ceremony, or work with others. You can also open Sacred Space any time you feel you need to have a little help and security for what you are doing. Prayers often have a religious meaning, and, if a specific religion is important to you, certainly also welcome in the Great Spirit with whom you work. Prayers can be individual and personal. When doing fire ceremonies with others, they are also collective and full of intention. Say your prayers out loud so they can be heard. Pachamama and the other spirits would prefer not to read your mind.

Sample Invocation (based on one found in Michael Harner's *The Way of the Shaman)*:

To the winds of the South, to the spirits of the South, Great Serpent, Amaru. Wrap your coils of light around us. Teach us to shed the past the way you shed your skin. Teach us to walk softly on the Earth. Teach us to flow.

To the winds of the West, to the spirits of the West, Mother-Sister Jaguar, Chocochinchi. Protect our medicine space. Teach us the way of peace. Teach us the ways to connect to others and to our land. Show us the way beyond death.

To the winds of the North, to the spirits of the North, Hummingbird, Kenti, Grandmothers, Grandfathers, Ancient Ones, come and warm your hands by our fire. Whisper to us in the wind. We honor you who have come before us and you who will come after us. Show us the structure of our path.

To the winds of the East, to the spirits of the East, Great Eagle, Condor, Vulture, Apuchin, come to us from the place of the rising

Sun. Keep us under your wings. Show us how to soar. Teach us to fly with the Great Spirit. Protect our Medicine space.

Mother Earth, Pachamama. Hold us sweetly in your arms, dear Mother, as we gather to honor you, and to thank you for your strength and support. We welcome all our relations: the Stone People, the Plant People, the Standing Talls, the Four Leggeds, the Two Leggeds, the Creepy Crawlies, the Finned, the Furred, and the Winged Ones.

Father Sun, Grandmother Moon, the Star Nations. Great Spirit, you who are known by a thousand names and you who are the unnamable One, we welcome your warmth, your love, and your wisdom. Teach us to journey with the Great Spirit.

Opening Your Wiracocha

Another way to create Sacred Space around yourself is to open your Wiracocha, your Light Body. Awareness of your own energy field, and the strength and protection it provides you, allows you to journey safely and work with others in healing. Your Wiracocha creates a clear space, and it holds that space for you, while you work. Sit or stand. Bring your hands toward the Earth, your palms touching and fingers pointing down. Holding the intention of bringing the Earth's energy and your energy field up around you, your hands move from the Earth, up the center of your body, rising above your head. There, your hands separate and your arms move out and down to the sides, creating a bubble of energy around you. Repeat twice more, for a total of three times. To create this Sacred

Space around another person, instead of moving your arms out and down to your side, move your arms forward and around the other person. Your intent is to create a bubble of Earth energy and a bubble of your Light Body, around the other person. First, open your Wiracocha around yourself. Then, open it around another. When your ceremony is complete, close your Wiracocha by simply crossing your arms over your chest.

TWO

Mapping the Personal:
A New Way to Walk in the World

You will need: Three stones that sing to you (*i.e.,* three stones that you like); one additional, very special, stone; and a pretty cloth, measuring about 22" x 24", to hold your stones.

One of the first goals of the Shamanic practitioner is to be in Ayni, to walk in Ayni, and to practice Ayni. Ayni is simply defined as a mid-point or a place of harmony and balance. Ayni means being in "right relationship" but also encompasses much more than those words convey.

In walking in Ayni, one can walk in Three Worlds or Earth Archetypes or Forces of Nature. The first is the nether world, the underground/the belly of the Mother. It is that place where seeds grow, where stars are born, where babies are made; it is the cosmic world of the Hujupacha, the Lower World, and the unconscious. In traditional Chinese medicine, this is the place of the lower Tan Tien. The second is the Middle World. It is the place of current consciousness, and the world of exchange; it is the Kaypacha. It is also the middle Tan Tien or heart center. The Upper World, or Hanaqpacha, is where one aspires to be at peace with one's self and the world. This center, the place of the upper Tan Tien, or third eye, allows one to see from afar, gain perspective, and be in tune with one's Higher Self.

And, also in Ayni, there are two domains of energy: Heaven and Earth. In those domains are those whose consciousnesses interact to order to exercise presence in the <u>now</u>. Ayni is walking in the world being fully present in <u>now</u>.

The work of the medicine people of the high Andes is an Earth - and Fire-based cosmology, which is formed around an Ayllu, a group of people that come together for sacred work and who work in synchronicity. They pay attention to the work when it happens. The cosmology honors, and works with, Pachamama, Mother Earth. It also works with the Santa Tierras, the ancient spirits of the land. In this cosmology, you will create a Mesa, a traveling altar. The stones in your Mesa hold the history of the Earth, and they hold the energetic lines, the Cekes, from the place of their beginning. Where you live now, you have created a Ceke, an energy line. Where you have visited, you have created a Ceke. Some of these Ceke lines dissipate over time, and some stay with you. Through this work, we weave a container of Ceke filaments of light, and these filaments bring us to the ayllu, the collective of Shamanic practitioners, past and present, who teach and support us.

This cosmology works within three worlds. First is the Hujupacha, the Lower World. This is the level where soul retrieval takes place and is the garden we never left. Second is the Kaypacha, the Middle World. This is level of consensual reality, the "real" world." Third is the Hanaqpacha, the Upper World. This is the level of Spirit, the place from which we source. Within these worlds, we also explore three forces of Nature. The first symbolic force is Amaru, the serpent eating her tail, the symbol

of transformation and transforming, that which moves life from
season to season. Amaru, shedding her skin, circular, recreating
shows us how to flow freely and easily through life's challenges.
Amaru is also in our bodies as we metabolize food, feed our
relations, and invest our affections, our love. Amaru is in the
Hujupacha. The second symbolic force of nature is Chocochinchi,
a Jaguar that stipulates everything is constantly interacting and
everything in the Universe works around affinities. Nothing stands
alone. Everything is connected. Therefore, a grain of sand has the
memory of creating. When healing takes place, it is a trans-level
occurrence. Because our rationality applies only to what we
see, not to what we do not see, many inter-relations are missed.
Vibrations are frequencies we do not see. With Chocochinchi, we
are connected as much to the past as to the future, even though
we can see only the past. Chocochinchi can be seen as a mythic
feline, allowing the Shaman the legs to move from the world
of spirit to matter, and providing the medicine of knowing your
relationship with yourself in its temporal nature. Chocochinchi is
in the Kaypacha, the heart center, that place where nothing is as
it seems. The third symbolic force of nature is Apuchin, a winged
being, who gives vision and is the Earth's architect. Everything in
the Universe has emanated out of a *vision*. Vision informs creating
and it recreates itself over and over. But, there may be a time at
which the vision breaks and there is a quantum shift. When all the
elements come together, there is a shift. There may come a time
when you are no longer the same. For the Shaman, a "vision" of
the future helps with this shift. It is more than being in Ayni; it is
also about seeing that all that you can grow into depends upon your
temporal nature. What we tend to do and to see happens in linear

"time." In this work, the past and the future blend into the <u>now</u>.
You "see" with a new and expanded vision.

Western society emphasizes the needs and wants of individuals
over the needs and wants of the collective. We are driven into the
future by our need to acquire more money and things, to have a
new car, a new house, new clothes, etc. This temporal view does
not allow vision in our "care" of the planet and those with whom
we share it. Because they do not move, it is okay with many to
cut down the trees, blow up the mountains, and drill into the land.
Because they do not speak in a language most of us understand, it
is okay with many to kill other living beings at will or subject other
forms of life to our purposes. There is no transformative fire in the
present. There is no time to have a vision of that which we wish to
become, our very own vision of ourself and our role on this planet.
This cosmology walks out of time and places community before
individuals. What is good for the city is good for the state; what
is good for the state is good for the nation; what is good for the
nation is good for the planet; what is good for the planet is good
for the individual.

As you take the first steps on this path, you will shed the
past. You will shed those things that block your flow. You will
energetically illuminate things that block your flow and transform
your wounds so your stones can hold them. The wound becomes
the power in the stone, a sacred item, a Kuya. These Kuyas are
the foundation of your Healer's Mesa. First, you will recover your
past. The Shaman takes the past to the fire so it can evolve, change,
transform. For example, the energy that allowed you to be a good
student many years ago allows you to exercise presence and be

something else today. Second, you will express presence. You learn to be aware of what "is" and to be comfortable in your own skin. Third, you will be claimed by vision. This new "vision" changes your way of coping with the world. Because you will no longer be driven by scarcity, you can create and claim a vision of the best "you" possible.

An individual who leads a life of service is a Shaman. Others, who are driven by personal gain, are sorcerers. Shamans map and understand the personal and the becoming of the collective. We are here to remember, to clear, and to embody. When we pray for ourselves or for others, we ask that we, or the others, come into the healed state. To access that healed state, you need to be there yourself. You need to be in Luminous Awareness, in the Shamanic state, out of linear time. There, we can perceive our own light body, our Luminous Body. That field collects density as life events occur. Your mother's life events, even while you were in utero, as well as all past-life density, colors the way you are seen in the world. This has very much to do with the Lower World, the garden we have never left. You work with the Pacharinas, the sacred springs, and the flow of energy for the Universe, coming from the East. If our fields are blocked, the flow cannot come in clearly.

In Luminous Awareness, you set aside the ego. You put aside all the "shoulds" and are present with Spirit. You work with Yanantin, a complementary coming together of what seems to be opposites: female/male, night/day, black/white. You work with awareness. You work with awareness of your Light (or Luminous) Body and become aware of what *is* in a completely different way—just what *is*.

There are many ways to move into Luminous Awareness. Practice the two methods covered next and see which helps you shift easily to this clear way of seeing. In the first method, begin by placing your palm on your thigh. Become aware of your hand. Become aware of your thigh. Become aware of the space between your hand and your thigh—that is the space of Luminous Awareness. Practice awareness of this space between your thigh and your hand. Practice awareness. Being aware of this small space between your palm and your thigh expands your view of what is and how it fits into conceptual reality. The second method creates awareness at different levels. To begin, stand in the world and be aware. Out loud say what you see: *I see . . . I see . . . I see . . . .* What you hear: *I hear . . . I hear . . . I hear.* What you smell: *I smell . . . I smell . . . I smell.* What you taste: *I taste . . . I taste . . . I taste.* What you sense: *I sense . . . I sense . . . I sense* (the fullness of the experience, just Be-ing in the moment). <u>This is a very literal exercise without judgment, just what *is.*</u>

In this sense of Be-ing, in Luminous Awareness, there are orders of relationship or levels of engagement with the worlds, and this is a horizontal pattern: awareness, touching, embracing. First, you experience Tinqui (pronounced "tin-quee"), that first awareness of something, that first awareness that there is something else there. This is basic investigation of the space, like a wolf would investigate. Then, you experience Tupay (pronounced "too-pigh") an awareness that the two fields are touching, getting closer. Tupay is how you personally confront what you experience through awareness. Third, you notice Take (pronounced "ta-kay"), a complete engagement, the joining of the passion of embracing

wholly and fully. Create this sense of Be-ing in Luminous
Awareness by saying to yourself: "Tinqui, Tupay, Take."

The Shaman's way of seeing is a kind of "squinty-eyed" and
asks: "What is there beyond the consensual reality?" The Shaman
looks at the world with Luminous Awareness through the three
Centers of Engagement (the Lower, Middle, and Upper Worlds),
and the three ways of looking at the world (Amaru, Chocochinchi,
and Apuchin). To begin practicing this way of seeing, we begin
at the lowest level, Amaru. Always in Ayni, in balance, open your
belly into the Earth. In Amaru, everything is as it is, and there
you may find the area of right action or Llancha (pronounced
"yan-cha). Then move your vision to Chocochinchi, the rainbow
light warrior of Jaguar in the Middle World. There you gain a sense
of connectivity. In the Kaypacha, the heart center, we find a state
of unconditional love (or munay, pronounced moon-aye) as Jaguar
gets into the emotion of things. In Jaguar, nothing is as it seems. In
Jaguar, there is emotion, projection, and drama. We do not have to
be locked in the "drama" created by Jaguar. Step out to Amaru, the
literal, or to Apuchin, the vision.

Say: "Tuku munay nina," I come to you with unconditional love.
Say: "Tuku yachi niok," I come to you with the total power of
mind.
Say: "Tuku munay niok," I come to you with the total power of
love.
Say: "Tuku hanchi niok," I come to you with the total power of
right action.

23

Pronunciation guide: "too-koo moon-aye neen-a, too-koo ya-chee nee-ock, too-koo moon-aye nee-ock, too-koo haunch-ee nee-ock"

Then create a vision or framework from afar—the place to which Condor/Eagle is leading us. The vision draws us as we draw it. Now, we come into right relationship with our community, our family, our world, and ourselves. In the eye of the Eagle, discerning, detaching with warmth so we have an understanding of what is and how it works in the world, come into the Upper World of our "Be-coming," the Hanaqpacha.

Creating a Nature Painting

To begin this transformative journey and create the Healer's Mesa, you begin with a simple Mandala, a Nature Painting created not from sand but, rather, with items you find in nature. This "painting" is an animistic representation of your life's landscape. Nature paintings represent your own (or a client's) life at the time of their creation. Working with the Nature Painting allows you to give up to the Divine the themes you place in them. You first bring the literal, Amaru, to the painting. The elements involved then begin their journey of transformation. Then you begin to work at the mythic or soul level of engagement where language is ceremony and images. There is no difference between you and the image. You make a change in your Nature Painting, and as the painting changes, so do the themes in your life. Nature paintings are created, used, and then destroyed, usually in a 12 to 48 hour period. All elements used are returned to nature, buried, or taken to the fire in ceremony.

To create a Nature Painting:

- Go into Luminous Awareness and find a space in nature that feels appropriate to you. This should be a beautiful place or a place that feels that it fits with the issue on which you are working. Open Sacred Space. Open your Wiracocha.

- Create a circle on the Earth. This circle will act as a "spirit catcher." The outer edge contains the energy in the painting and is created by making an outline by either drawing it on the ground with a stick or your finger, or using natural elements (*e.g.*, sticks, flowers, etc.) to define it. This circle catches the spirit of the energy in your life that you want to transform. Draw your hand around that spirit catcher a few times to really catch the spirit of what you are working with and instill it in the circle.

- Place items from nature in the circle to represent what you are expressing or feeling. Let that spirit begin to speak to you. This is not a mental exercise; let it evolve and inform you. As you feel what you want to create, begin to notice natural elements around you. Find items that represent or symbolize your stories, your passions, and your life. If you are working with stones, place them in the part of the circle representing that with which you are working. Try not to think about this process too much. Let yourself be guided by your instincts. Truly feel and sense.

- As you think about the themes or issues in your life that you wish to transform, hold a leaf or flower or stem (or other natural item) to represent that issue. Talk about your issue while holding this item. Blow your issue into the item using your sacred breath. When you feel ready to move to the next theme, place the item you are holding in the painting where it feels right to you.

Go back to your painting several times during the next 12-48 hours. This is your palette as you work in each of the four directions, but it can also be your palette as you work on other issues in your life or as you help others work through their issues. The Nature Painting is a tool to work with your problems. When issues or challenges arise, put them in a Nature Painting. Keep the work at the mythic level, not the literal. Do not let yourself get caught in the story. In this process, Pachamama will help mulch the energy as you are giving these themes up to the Divine.

The South: Amaru, the Snake

In the work of the South, you will be working with issues of personal woundedness. In the Nature Painting you will create for the South, include themes you wish to heal, which will allow you to transform. In this Nature Painting, you will include three sources of your woundedness and create a display of what is claiming you and how. The Nature Painting includes four levels of engagement:

literal, symbolic, mythic, and essential. Reflect on this energy. From where did it come? Where is the memory in your body? Take some time to figure this out. You may want to journey and ask for help in sorting out the three themes you need to include at THIS time in your life.

Work with the Nature Painting is at the levels of (A) Literal and Symbolic, and (B) Mythic and Energetic. Western cultures go from A to B. The Shaman moves from B to A. The quickest change in consciousness, and in the Luminous Body, occurs at the energetic level. Density, or a block in the flow, will show up in one of the seven chakras or one of the three centers in this cosmology. When you first create your Nature Painting, you are working at the literal and symbolic level. As the painting changes, it does so at the energetic level. As that energy enters your painting and transforms it, you also are transformed.

Using broad themes, outline the story of your life in linear time. What year were you born? Who was important then? Who was important at other times in your life? Go into nature and spend some time drawing your life. Begin by writing down the year you were born. Add years of key events in y our life until you reach the <u>now</u>. Jot in those blanks what you remember about what you were doing. This is a standard way to start an autobiography.

An example is:

1953—Born in New York City
1956—Moved to Buffalo
1961—Moved to Pittsburgh

1962—Moved to Philadelphia

1964—Moved to Harrisburg

1965, 1966—Moved within Harrisburg; variety of entry level jobs

1970—Graduated from high school

1972—Moved to Champaign

Various secretarial type jobs as a student

1973—Moved to Urbana; married

1974—Earned Bachelor of Science degree; various office jobs

1980—Divorced

1983—Moved to Champaign

1987—Earned Master of Science degree; professional position held for 25 years

1990—Remarried

1995—Death of youngest sister

2006—Death of middle sister; changed careers

And, of course, all the details of life are in between those markers. The issues, themes, and those things that were recurring, often stand out when writing out major life events in this way. Look for those themes. Those themes may also contain stories that you need to release. In the example, for instance, it is fairly easy to spot the first one: moving.

Take your time when working with the stories of your life. At the end of the process, you will begin to know that you are more than your stories. Although your stories may have created the "you" of now, they no longer need to define you or direct your future. Some of these issues/themes are to go into your Nature Painting. From there, you will help to move them out of your Luminous Body and into the stones representing them at the mythic level. By transforming your issues in the painting, you also are transformed at the physical level. This is the Shamanic way of moving from the mythic to the literal.

The exercise of writing your life story as a river allows you to recover the past and, at the same time, become aware of the flow—Amaru. All that was past was taken to the fire and evolved, changed. That process allowed me, and can allow you, to express presence in the world in which we live and be claimed by a vision beyond any I had before embarking on this path.

These sources of woundedness, churning around in a state of emotional chaos, can be considered as a "lidded/hidden" emotion. Eckhart Tolle refers to this as an "anger body." The anger body takes over and reacts in ways the aware body would not do. The hidden emotions can create reactions to situations that often have little or nothing to do with the present. This process can create a continuing cycle of re-wounding and often prevents a person from reaching a healed state.

The key to moving on and losing the ability of the stories to control the reaction is to transform that "lidded emotion," into a positive "reaction." Creation of a positive reaction leads to "joy." Joy leads to a sense of control over the situation/action and to a sense of understanding. Understanding can lead one to prayer or meditation about the emotion and deeper awareness. With that deeper awareness, one can move into the healed state. The key is in developing awareness. When caught up in the emotion, all that is known is that energy. In this work, we will learn to shift levels of awareness and, by so doing, create the awareness we need to transform.

We only have responsibility for our own actions and reactions. In this cosmology, you do not blame others for what happens. When you create your life, you are in control. When you create your life, through all of the events in your life, you are in control. When you are in control, there is no need for fear. Many of our current reactions are based in fear. Fear of change. Fear of loss. Fear of death. Sometimes the fear is about the loss of others who are important to us and to our stories. Our parents, partners, children, and friends can fuel our fear. However, you are the only one responsible for yourself. What others lose, or when and how they die, is their cycle. Their cycle is also one of birth and death. Death before birth. Birth before death. In this cosmology, it is believed that the soul has planned several places where it can exit. Other souls also know when it is time for them to leave and under which circumstances for the lessons they are learning. This way of thinking does not necessarily make it easier to face the deaths of those we love, especially if it is a violent or early death. But, knowing that there are many potential exit points for us, and others, offers comfort.

Remember: you only see what you know. You do not see what you do not know. If you see something large and shiny flying in the sky, you assume it is an airplane and go on with your day. If you see what looks like a tiny person with wings, you assume your eyes are wrong and what you saw was a big bug or bird. Be aware of what you see by using all your senses. Find ways to engage in perceptual shifts consistently. When looking from the level of a

Snake on the ground, you see what is on the ground. When you see from the perspective of a Jaguar you see what is on the ground and around you at a slightly higher level. When you see from the height of the Eagle in flight, you have a very broad view. Shifting your perception from the level of Amaru, the flow, to that of Jaguar or Eagle, will be discussed more in later chapters. For the time being, think about the Pacha—an interval of time and space. Each interval includes a physical, mental, emotional, spiritual, and quantum mechanical element working in tandem. Every Pacha is multi-faceted and helps to move you through time and space. Pachas usually move in seven-year cycles.

Creating Kuyas

The word Kuya means to love unconditionally. We need to change the energetic composition of our woundedness to a source of power so it becomes a Kuya—a place of unconditional love, and, therefore, a sacred item. These situations/facts that are not healed try to find any kind of opportunity to emerge so they can heal. Something from your past can (and most likely, will) show up because it needs healing. Everything in the Universe seeks balance—a state of congruence—oneness—Ayni. So, any source of woundedness that has not been healed will knock on your door until you listen to it and heal. Sometimes it feels as if a hammer hits you, and at other times it is subtler. However, the issue will repeat and repeat over and over in the choices you make until you recognize it as an opportunity for healing and energetic growth.

Everything engages in an affinity. You divorce the first spouse and get another partner who is the same—the old wound opens back, still needing healing. These affinities dwell in all four domains. To address the woundedness, you must heal in all four domains: the physical/mental, emotional, spiritual, and quantum mechanical.

You need to understand what the healing is about: recovering a missing attribute, being at peace, a sense of the Universe patting you on the back. Healing is *not* about fixing things. It is about *wholeness.* If you think about terminal illness, like cancer, you cannot really change that, but you *can* change the mental, emotional, and spiritual aspects of that illness. You were born with a blueprint of the perfect, physical you. That blueprint exists in your Luminous Body. *Healing is allowing your body to remember its own physical, emotional, and spiritual state of perfection*. The best healing is holistic in a way that involves everything. For the *transformation* process, there needs to be a new mind/heart set, a new perception. The embodiment is fulfilling again the new transformation. What does being "healthy" feel like for you? You are no longer the person who was sick. You are someone else. Embrace the healed state.

Real healing comes when the body remembers its own healed state.

Whole-heartedly embrace your *healed state*. Love begets love. Fear begets fear. Focus. Exercise presence. Be available for an act of personal power. Surrender, embracing the mystery. What will take you into a progress of change, your capacity to exercise selfless love, is called tukuymun nayniyok (too-koo-mon nigh-nee-ook).

The journey is to "map" your personal stories. As you do so, the stories merge into the collective, and things move to oneness. For power to be available, the power to act with unconditional love is a requirement. To move into the healed state, create something that represents the themes you wish to release in your life and place each of those themes into a Nature Painting. After each issue transforms in the painting, remove that representation and place it in the fire with the intention of letting go. What you place in the Nature Painting can be as simple as a sheet of paper with the words expressing the general idea of your issue, or as elaborate as parts of plants tied with colored ribbons and decorated with flowers to represent both the problem, and the healing you wish to occur. Always, a stone can be used to take on this theme and carry it for you. The power of your intention can focus work with the theme(s) in the Nature Painting. Meditate on it/them. Through meditation, stillness, prayer, and gratitude, track it/them from all levels of awareness. With the power of your intent can come healing, transformation, and the full embodiment of your life. Attend to the *energy* of that/those theme(s), and how it/they has/have manifested in your life.

To become a person of power, you move through levels of awareness and experience. First, you must acquire a body of knowledge. For example, once you embrace the song, it opens up and gives you information. It may be written in temples or in mountains, but it must be discovered by you to make the experience yours. Make the song and the experiences your own.

Second, move into the collective through rites of passage. For example, after acquiring knowledge through attending school, a graduation ceremony (a rite of passage) is held to recognize the knowledge acquired. Rites of passage recognize personal growth through experience. Third, a body of ritual allows you to be a part of consensual reality and at the same time embrace a heightened state of reality. That heightened state of reality shifts your awareness and experience into a place of power. The Shaman's Path gives you the knowledge, the rites of passage, and the tools of ritual (the Nature Painting), and ceremony (the fire) to move you into the healed state.

Creating the Healer's Mesa

Map the personal. Beyond your role in the world, regain the knowingness of yourself. Master the personal. Your Mesa is the pathway to connect with the medicine tradition and embodies aspects of the collective that pertain to you.

Look at your stories. In each, you play the role of Victim, Perpetrator, or Savior/Rescuer. The Shaman says we leave that cycle now. The Perpetrator comes out of fear and exercises power for gain. You need to come face to face with each archetype of woundedness (Persecutor, Victim, Rescuer) and defeat each archetype. Then you bring in a new archetype of right relationship, groundedness, so you are no longer claimed by your fears but by your life. Release those models of behavior that are not "growing corn." These old archetypes do not work. They do not support growth. They do not support Ayni.

There are also three centers in the body where we exchange energetic information with the world. In this cosmology, these are:

- forehead—Yachay, the Upper World;

- heart—Munay, the Middle World; and

- belly—Llankay, the Lower World.

The belly digests, mulches, transforms. As Amaru, the Serpent, it is the force of nature in charge of moving, it is circulation—it brings rivers to the ocean and accepts that after summer is fall. Amaru regenerates and brings life to new beginnings. Amaru is found in the belly.

The body is the reflection of the land. In Western cosmology, the mind and body are disconnected, yet we *are* in our bodies. Your biological lineage (an expression of your parents and ancestors), expressions of the collective (values that may not pertain to this time), and your karmic lineage (psychological/social) depict who you are. The Inka believe creation is happening all at once. As a wheel connected by its spokes, awareness allows you to remember all at once. When you do healing at the mythic (ritual) level, you can penetrate into your higher senses. The journey is creating a meaningful relationship with life.

Cycles of life, or Pachas, move rhythmically without our help. We are born. Various things are going to happen. We are going to die. What we can change are the attributes. When the Shaman dreams his or her day into being, the vision is at the essential or

35

spiritual level. That level of awareness, the essential, organizes the mythic level. The mythic is that place where our collective stories live and grow and change. The mythic level organizes the symbolic level. From mythology comes the symbol of an angel, a God, a Victim, a Rescuer. The mythic level then organizes the literal, *e.g.,* the book in your hand, or the outside temperature. The essential level, a level above that of Eagle/Condor/Apuchin, is the place where everything speeds up. It is the place where your stories transform and no longer bind you. To tap into the essential, the Shaman uses the mythic level through ritual and ceremony. The wormhole, that place where everything speeds up on its way to transformation, is at the mythic/the ritual level of awareness. To create a meaningful relationship with your own life, get out of the literal.

The belly, Llankay, is the way your body transforms, creates, and feeds life at all levels (literal, symbolic, mythic, essential). When you heal at the essential level, you are informing and healing all the other levels at the same time. This is why we work first with the lowest chakra holding stuck energy. When the lower level is cleared, the others also clear. The collective stories and mythology of our culture, as well as both our biological and karmic lineages, help us to understand who we are. When you know your "guiding myths," you begin to process and clear your Luminous Body at the essential level.

The middle center, Munay, is the heart sense of connection. Everything we unfold ourselves into is Munay, the ability to open up. From a place of unconditional love, the heart center opens and allows the Shaman to love without expectation of return. This kind of loves creates clarity and connection, and allows the Shaman to know that nothing is as it seems.

Yachay, the upper center, is your intellect, your wisdom, experiences to which your Higher Self is connected. Yachay is the knowledge of a large repository of experiences. Open your crown to access your Yachay. Yachay grows corn with what you know and converts it to a larger medicine lineage. Because we live in ego, the literal, we forget what the healed state is. Yachay reminds us where we need to be going and growing.

Our bodies contain all these memories: literal, symbolic, mythic, and essential. All are in Yachay, Munay, and Llankay. And, to further complicate matters, all these memories can be found in our past, our present, or our future lives. Find these memories at each level in your Nature Painting. At the very least, work with memories from this lifetime.

To begin, first create Sacred Space. Go into ritual by going on a journey with the *intent* of contacting your Higher Self and guides. Then, ask your Higher Self. Ask your guides. Go into a trancelike state and then move into the sound of your rattle. Be as impersonal as possible, at the same time being personable in interactions. But, in matters of the heart, do not take things personally. Develop a more "negotiable" ego state. Source from a different place than your ego. The ego is easily hurt. When you are more flexible, you develop a more observing ego. With that more observing ego, there is no room for judgment, position, opinion, and defending the position. Judgment, position, opinion, and possession are the ego. Life is about *being* when it comes to the personal. Your opinions/judgments are found in a reflection of others. They are part of your personal Shadow, parts you do not like but find in others. Righteousness can create separation, so look at that with an open heart and be *negotiable*. Do not take the self too personally. Develop an observing ego. Do not create judgments about others because that creates separation. The judgment prevents you from "seeing." Without judging what you see, find what is practical for you in the <u>now</u>. Hold that space and contain it in your heart.

To summarize:

1. Do not take anything too seriously.

2. Develop an observing ego.

3. Practice innocence.

4. Be open and available.

5. Play. Play harder!!

A Pacha uses the energy of the land and what grows there in cyclical form. Simple examples are the seasons and cycles of life as beings move from birth to death. Pachamama, often just referred to as the Earth Mother, is more accurately the Mother of the Universe. Pachamama uses the energy of the Earth/Universe to create cycles in living.

Kausay is a vibration, a life force. A Kausay Pacha is wired to our physiology as the Kundalini energy of our bodies, and, at the same time, it is wired to the ley lines, the meridians, of the Earth and of the Universe. The vibration of the Earth and of the Universe connects us to the planet, to each other, and to other beings. Just as a plucked string on a guitar will cause other nearby strings to vibrate, the energy of this vibration informs those around us, as well as ourselves. We are fed by Kausay Pacha (the land), by Kausay Wayra (the air), and by Kausay Kanchay (the light). Light is the ultimate primordial organizing principal. Light dictates how time will unfold. The passage of the Sun creates time. When you understand that passage, you connect with time. Whenever we shift through ceremony, we need to move through light, air, and Earth.

Amorphic fields create layers of the aura. These layers are in the essential domain. When you create Sacred Space with intention, your Luminous Body opens up. Your aura expands. Your senses are more acute. There is, therefore, more room for information. Our physical bodies are attuned to our consensual reality. In Sacred Space, your Luminous Body expands, and, it no longer sees only consensual reality. Our vision expands.

Creating a Shaman's Lineage Stone

If you do not have a teacher but, instead, are completing this work on your own or with friends, you may create a special stone to use while doing the work outlined in the following chapters. This stone will also tie your Mesa together and give it a sense of completion as you complete the work of the North. You will use it as you complete all the exercises with other stones. At the end of the path, you will create a special ceremony for just this stone.

39

Find a most beautiful stone. Clear it with Florida Water, and place it in a Nature Painting outside. Let it sit outside for a full lunar month. Time the process so that you begin at a new moon. Occasionally, check on the stone and see how the painting has changed. When the moon is again new, remove it from the Nature Painting and move into Luminous Awareness. Hold your newly created Lineage Stone and welcome it into your life. Find or make a beautiful cloth about two-feet square. This cloth will hold your stones safely when you are not using them. In Peru, this cloth is called a *Mestana,* and you can also find cloths by this name for sale from various sources on line. Use it to hold your stones and other items as you begin the process of creating sacred Kuyas for yourself.

Exercise. The following steps describe the process of working with stones to transform issues in your life that have created blocks. Blocks may be things that hold you in an inappropriate relationship or job; things that keep you from discovering your true purpose; or just a way of being in the world that leaves you feeling unsatisfied.

First, find three stones that have meaning for you. When choosing stones to include in your Mesa, your personal altar, select those that "speak" to you in some way. Perhaps you have a rock on your shelf from a special vacation you took as a child. There may be a place in nature you like to visit at which you "find" a stone that feels good. You may even go into a museum or store and find a stone to buy that makes you feel happy. These are all stones that "sing" to you and stones that may like to help you by holding your stories.

Then, find a beautiful place on your land. This is a place you will go to "sit" with your stones, to journey, to work with the energy that will transform. This will be called your "sit spot." There, create a circular Nature Painting, your Nature Painting. Make a boundary with biodegradable material. Leave the east open—that is where the flow of all new energy will enter.

1. Open space by calling in the spirits in whatever way is comfortable for you.

2. Enter Luminous Awareness.

3. Place your three stones in the painting.

4. Draw your life as a river using paper and crayons. Take some time with this part of the process. Use the outline you created earlier and begin to fill in more blanks. Write down important dates and events in your life in the appropriate years. Where were you born? Who was important in your life in those early years? What is your earliest memory? When did you start school? Who were your friends? Your teachers? Add key events: graduations, marriages, divorces, births, and deaths of loved ones, including pets. Be as complete as you can be. This river of your life flows and contains your stories. Those stories helped you be the person you are now. Some of these themes or stories you know you no longer need to hold.

5. Choose three incidences in life that have informed you greatly. These are themes that are unfinished business for

you. You are going to the origins of your wounds—where did *that* begin?

If working with others, choose a partner with whom you are comfortable sharing information about your life. If you are doing this exercise by yourself, use a doll or stuffed toy as your "witness." The one who listens is the Witness holding the space, not the fixer but the listener. The other talks out his/her issue, so the listener really gets a strong sense of the wounding. When all of the hurt is remembered (or as much as can be at that point in time), blow that one issue into a stone. Dredge up all the emotion into your body and blow into the stone a second time. Do this three times. This is Yana chaqui, the transmission of energy from one object to another. This pulls the theme out of your energy field and places it into the stone where it is held and eventually will be transformed.

6. Using a pendulum, check your chakras (for complete instructions see Chapter 6). Start with the first chakra and ask which chakra is discharging (going counter clockwise) to deal with this issue. If working with a partner, your partner will hold your stone in his/her non-dominant hand and check the chakras while you, the client, take relaxing breaths on the floor. This helps the mind to disengage. If there is more than one chakra involved, work first on the lowest one involved. Work on the lowest usually clears them all. If you are working alone, use your *intent* to check each chakra as you focus on the issue with which you are working.

7. If you are working alone, read the instructions for working
   with a partner. Then, lie down and place the Lineage
   Stone you created earlier in this chapter (or a stone from a
   Shaman's Mesa) and the stone holding your issue, on the
   culprit chakra, the lowest chakra discharging. The stones
   should touch each other. Begin to journey. Go to the lower
   world and ask Huascar to hold your neck and help you
   release this energy into the stone. You will feel a sense of
   deep relaxation when the process is complete. If working
   with a partner, your partner will use his/her rattle counter
   clockwise over the chakra to "tease" the energy out. Rattle
   counter-clockwise over the stones. The energy is rattled and
   teased out of your chakra and into the stone. Your partner
   will hold the back of your neck and very gently massage
   those indentations on either side at the base of your skull.
   He/she will ask you to breathe in through your nose and
   out through your mouth. Really go to that issue blown into
   the stone. Feel the stone. Ask that the energy of the issue
   be drawn out and held by the stone. Again, your partner
   (or Huascar) will rattle counter clockwise over the stones
   and release stuck energy into the Earth. Again, your partner
   holds your neck, while you move into the issue. This
   process may be repeated several times as the issue shifts
   from your Luminous Body into the stone. Let your breath
   flow as the issue is pulled into the stone. When the work
   is done, whether by a partner or by Huascar, you will feel
   a difference in your body, or notice a difference with your
   breath. Your partner may ask you how you are feeling. Stay
   there, breathing quietly, until you feel sure the issue has
   shifted. Re-check the chakras. This is work at the energetic

level. When the stone is returned to the painting, the issue is taken to the mythic level. Repeat the process with each of the three stones.

8. Enter Luminous Awareness and go back to your Nature Painting. As you walk, look for flowers, leaves, or other items of nature to add to the painting. Place the stones back in the painting and place those newly found items around them. Let the stones rest overnight. Let them sit in the painting. Clear your Lineage Stone with Florida Water (to clear stones, or anything else for that matter, in this cosmology, a light spritz of Florida Water from the mouth, not a spray bottle, does the trick) and return it to your *Mestana*.

9. We will come back to these stones after they have rested overnight.

For the past day and night, the three stones that contain three themes or wounding's of your life's story have been transforming in the Nature Painting. Go back to the Nature Painting you have created. It is time to leave those stories behind as they have been imprinted on the stones. The stones will carry that part of you now. You can now move forward without those burdens. Sit quietly for a few moments by the Nature Painting. Observe it carefully. Has anything changed? Are the stones in the same place you left them? Has anything left your painting? Has anything been added?

When picking up your stones and clearing the Nature Painting, enter Luminous Awareness. Listen, see, smell, taste, and sense that space between each stone. Ask the stone: "Are you to return with me to my Mesa?" Sometimes they say "no." Honor their request if they wish to stay. Give gratitude to the land. Dismantle the painting so that no one could tell it was ever there. Save some of the sticks, grasses, and flowers for the fire and scatter the rest. Your three stones now hold your stories for you and have become Kuyas, sacred stones. The Lineage Stone you used, too, holds all the stories. You have now created the first fourth of your Healer's Mesa.

Create a Despacho ceremony (see Chapter Eight) to move the new "you" into Ayni with the <u>now</u> and to welcome your newly created Kuyas. Make an offering of tobacco or sage or lavender to the fire and clear your three centers of exchange (belly, heart, forehead). Then offer, with prayers of gratitude, the burnables from your Nature Painting. As you rise from the fire, move your newly created Mesa over the fire in a clockwise way seven times. Then place your Despacho in the hot coals. Turn and walk away from the fire.

Now, you will begin to walk the path of the Shaman. You are no longer your stories, and your Luminous Body is changing its vibration. Every day you practice, you will move along the Shamanic Path and find yourself closer to your healed state.

Exercise. The following steps are suggestions for following the Shamanic Path:

1. Every day, assemble your day. Begin each morning with a simple meditation. Close your eyes and begin to rattle.

Go into Luminous Awareness. Let the rattle take you out of your body and on a brief journey into your day. Visualize your schedule. See positive outcomes for any potential difficulty. Track your day. Is your route to work long and full of delays? See your route free of obstacles with a perfect parking place at the end. Is your boss too hard a taskmaster? Are your colleagues annoying? See your boss praising your work, and your colleagues being helpful. Children or spouse causing you conflicts? See you interactions as positive, fluid, loving. Move through your day in its ideal form. When you are done, sit for a few moments in contemplation. Take a deep breath. Let consensual reality bring you back.

2. Exercise presence; availability.

3. Fine-tune your *intent*, your drive, and your focus. Your perception governs your reality, but it is better for your focus to guide you. Let your focus govern your reality. *Intent*. When *intent* grows, you can do incredible things. When *intent* is *focused,* manifestation can happen. Shamanism is a path of service with *intention*.

4. Vision. Have a hawk's eye view of what will happen. See where you are in the world. Assemble your day around *stillness*. Pray. Exercise gratitude and appreciation.

There are two sources of information for who you are today: biological and karmic. The biological includes your DNA, guiding myths, core beliefs, and imprints. Karma is based on what you do and what you have done in the past. Whatever you do, the Earth writes a ceremony around it. This ceremony disconnects you from the biologic forces and can help you be claimed by a medicine lineage. Embracing the land through ceremony creates the medicine lineage.

The medicine lineage awakens us to realms of spirits. The voices of the forest become more audible to you. When you become one with nature, you might see the little people, energies emanating from the trees, and more! Our stones are transformed in our Mesa and become a representation of the medicine lineage. The stone becomes the mountain. You bring it to yourself in ceremony.

We want the biological and karmic lineages to stop forming us and instead use the medicine lineage to become an active co-participator in creation. The medicine lineage (1) ensures fertility, (2) creates Ayni, (3) creates well-being, and (4) creates light. Fertility allows us to be always nourished, always cared for, always fresh, always creating. Every Pacha has a peak, a sense of fruition, and you can craft almost anything with fertility. Fertility creates the means to survive and grow.

Ayni. Right relationship. Right exchange. Balance. Give back to the land, to God, what rightfully belongs to them. Create right relationship with everything, both spoken and unspoken. Bringing balance brings right relationship. For example, in a love relationship, you can serve yourself or serve the relationship. Serving the relationship better brings balance. Serve the experience. By doing so, it is no longer personal. How do you serve? How do you embody or create reciprocity? When you know what is yours, you take responsibility. When you know what is yours, there is no room for guilt. Take responsibility for Ayni. The ultimate Ayni is your responsibility to yourself. The effects of reciprocity are feeding your soul and embracing your heart. What are your duties to yourself? When they are clear, you can walk into the world and create Ayni for the world.

You cannot waste your time fixing things that cannot be fixed. Fixing deals with details. Healing addresses all the elements and gives the person a sense of wholeness. One awakens the memory of a healed state. Stay away from the cycle of Rescuer, Victim, and Perpetrator. Healing brings wholeness. Ceremonial space helps allow healing.

Everything gravitates toward light expressed through unconditional love. There is no particle in physics that does not move toward light. Dense energy may be due to a sickness or an imbalance, and it needs to be brought to the light to heal. In healing, recognize the density and allow that clogged energy to return to the light.

Recognize the personal, family, and collective mythologies by dialoguing with others. A core belief is your application of your guiding mythology. Core beliefs can be just yours, your family's, your neighborhood's, city's, country's, religion's, etc. For example, a fairly universal core belief is based on scarcity. Because you may "need" something later, you "save" it. The choices are: A. keep _____, or B. throw it out.

Where is the balance?

To change, become open to breaking the rules. Examine the source of your beliefs. Is it personal? Who is responsible? Your family? Your teachers? Your friends? You? Is this a collective belief? Collective beliefs inform countries, most often in religion or politics. For example, in Western culture, it was accepted for many years that men needed to be in control and women were to be subservient. Men were the providers; women were the nurturers. Men held property and could vote. Women did not. Men were priests. Women were not. There was (and in many places still is) a collective belief that the white race is superior to all other races. Racial superiority led to the acceptance of physical abuse in slavery, justified wars, and led to a wide variety of other beliefs about the place of people in the scheme of the Universe. Where did you "find" the beliefs that inform you?

Some personal beliefs may allow one to hide in low self-esteem or make one believe one has to do things for others. For example, if your father abused or was abused, a history of abuse is created. Do you believe this pattern is a rule that cannot be broken? Is abuse then inevitable? Is that a personal core belief? Or, can you make a change in the pattern? Some family beliefs are for joy! Not all beliefs are "bad" or need to be changed. <u>The key is to recognize where the belief or pattern originated and work with how it manifests in your life from there.</u>

Map the personal. What is the source of your reaction? Grab it. Then change it. These are human archetypes, and they can limit us. We need to create a new dialog with other Earth archetypes. *Choose your engagements carefully.*

There are various types of Earth Archetypes:

1. Archetype of Luminous Warrior. The Luminous Warrior practices peace and dares to speak her/his truth.

2. Archetype of the Sage. The Sage will articulate the wisdom of the land in a way it can be embraced.

3. Archetype of the Seer. The Seer shows you all the possible outcomes.

4. Archetype of the Dreamer. The Dreamer teaches you to be claimed by your vision.

5. Archetype of the Lover. The Lover is an individual who can express unconditional love in all relations and lives life to the fullest, fearlessly.

6. Archetype of the Goddess, Fertility, Connectivity. This is Mother Earth, Vesta, Minerva, Athena, and Hera.

The task for us is to map our guiding mythology, like the "hero" (have to do things right, bite your tongue, cannot hurt, bear up, etc.) who lives through suffering. We need to move from this old pattern into an Earth Archetype—into something that gives you an identity.

Whatever you do, there is a drive to create membership or a sense of belonging. Remember, we have been thrown out of the garden and disconnected from the Earth. The Hujupacha, the unconscious or dreamtime, shows up outside the grip of language, a place creation is happening . . . the land and underground. Energetically, we may have a "wounded womb." Shameful feelings about our sexuality, regardless of gender, have created a mythology, a way of understanding about notions of home, mother, and creation. In our traditions, we discovered the feminine and created a male god. To avoid pain, the Hujupacha, the unconscious, is where we go. Shattered parts of the soul go to the Mother. A lot of information/seeds go to see the light of day and reside in the territories of Hujupacha.

In the Hujupacha, there is a guide or a keeper named Muki (moo-key), a shape shifter. The Hujupacha is the collective unconscious and it is also the garden you never left. Part of it is personal for you. It is enchanted water, and it takes time to map. Muki is the guide who the Inka say helps you travel there. Each domain has a guide, a gatekeeper who gives you permission to travel there. We need to move to a waking dream state to journey.

Exercise. Learn to Journey. Turn off the phone; make sure you will not be disturbed. Lie down and get comfortable. You might cover your eyes with a cloth, a towel, or an eye pillow. Breathe deeply a few times and relax. Always set an intention for your journey. Always journey with intent. Open Sacred Space. State your intention out loud. In this first journey, set your intention to explore the Lower World with the help of Muki.

Begin to rattle or drum with a consistent and steady beat, or use a journey recording. When using a recording, its length determines the length of your journey. When you drum or rattle for yourself, you and your guide decide when it is time for you to come back. Close your eyes. Envision yourself standing on a hill. Look at your feet and hands. Who are you? Walk into a cave in the side of the hill. Surrender. Dive into the unknown. Not knowing is good medicine because it allows you to see better. Extend your hand to Muki. Leap into the unknown. Muki will keep you safe.

Go with the experience for five to ten minutes. Then come back the way you went in. Walk back to the hill. Look down at your hands and feet. Open your eyes. Who are you?

In the work of the South, we worked with Amaru. The energy of Amaru resets, sheds, like a snake all at once; Amaru makes change. Wind and ocean currents move rivers and create evaporation; evaporation creates rain; rain creates life. Regenerating and shifting moves us in different cycles and resides here, in our bellies. As we have been removed from the land, Amaru has been enclosed and trapped. It needs to be released to be in its full presence. Presence then allows healthier rebirth. Healthy rebirth allows you to embrace the fullness of life you need to gain the ability to change. The ability to change allows you to ride that wild horse and be dynamic. Being dynamic allows you to see all of your life's cycles. You may see different lifetimes in this lifetime. The ability to shape shift allows you to be fully available and shift. The energy of Amaru allows the change to occur without carrying the burden of the past. The Shamans of the high Andes call this Ayni Carpi, the reawakening of your Amaru.

In the work of the West, we move to Jaguar, Chocochinchi. Here everything in the Universe is interrelated and shows up as a web of all sorts of relations. We are our stories, our thoughts, and we are each other. When we go to the fire, we heal ourselves as well as all of our relationships. This can affect past, as well as future, relationships. Chocochinchi is seen as a luminous feline, and allows you to choose all of your relations and to see all your relations. Chocochinchi is the force of nature in its most primordial sense—emphasizing the connectedness of everything. Knowing the connection allows you/the Shaman to track the relation. The organizing principal of inner connectivity that allows you to sense the connection with everything is unconditional love. The more you are able to exercise unconditional love, the stronger the connectivity.

Belong to the land, not to your stories. The Jaguar needs to be reawakened so you can love with intensity and passion, and express the fullness of the awareness, the connectivity. Appreciation allows connection with others—read their thoughts—connect the energy—shift the whole to understanding. Appreciation allows you to understand what disempowers you and causes your fear. When you recognize what disempowers you, you can stop it from coming your way. It gives you a great range of responses to all kinds of situations.

In the East lies Apuchin, who is represented by the Eagle, the mythic vision, the sense of the collective and the pool of information that holds the collective. You can move to this pool and download information. Journey to the collective and bring information back into yourself. The answers to all your questions are there. Shut down your rational, ego-based mind and open your crown chakra and channel. The types of vision our ego state produces are responses to our scarcity mentality. As long as our visions are from the ego, the scarcity ideology cannot be healed. Mythic vision is larger. It is the process of creation and recreation. Apuchin already envisions the oak 100 years from today, berries 500 years from today, and what will be hundreds of years from now. The blueprint for creation you have to envision pertains not only to ego, based on what is missing in your life, but also that which fulfills your soul's purpose. That communion of everything allows you to experience life in a collective way and is a journey toward collectivity. Apuchin allows you to understand the vision that fulfills your soul.

Learn to weave the Amaru of the land into your belly. Feel how germination happens. Your medicine bag, your Mesa, becomes an altar. It embodies the journey on the medicine path as one develops a relationship with nature. Your Mesa is the living embodiment of your journey. It is also a compiler of energy, a receptacle for the cosmic energies. It grows and can become your alter ego. The ceremony that welcomes your stones into the collective transforms them into the lineage of the high Andes, and they become tools for healing. When the intent is placed in ceremony, the Mesa is activated, and it can be truly amazing. However, the ceremony is not what makes your stones Kuyas. What ultimately transforms your stones are your intent, your prayers, and the work you have done imprinting your stories.

Exercise. In ceremony, or with your intent, you can build bands of power, strength, and protection, with a rainbow braid at the crown. Sit quietly, breathing deeply for a few moments. Relax your body as your mind focuses on building beautiful bands of energy around your Wiracocha. On the right side, visualize gold for Father Sun. On the left side, visualize silver in honor of the Mother. The gold and silver flow up and around the legs and feet and weave between them creating power and strength. When they reach the torso they encircle the body, creating different colored bands of power. At the level of the sacral chakra, a band of black is created. This band transforms to red at the heart. At the throat, the waters of the Mother, the band is gold. At the third eye, the band is completely silver. As the bands move and swirl they become crystalline at the crown chakra. Imagine these bands of light around you, protecting you, and anchoring you to the work you do on this Earth.

As you continue with the work, it is nice to have spiritual help. Shamans often work with a power animal, and those animals provide assistance and guidance in healing work and other life issues. It is time to journey for a power animal to help you with this work.

Journey. Journey to the Hujupacha, to the Lower World, to find a power animal.

1. Intent: To find a power animal pertinent to the work you are doing now.

2. Drum or rattle. The beat helps you to go into Luminous Awareness. Focus on the sound to calm the mind and go to a deeper level of awareness. Go to a safe and beautiful

Sacred Space you know on this Earth. Find a place to
enter—a cave, between tree roots, under a stone, a crack
in the ground—you will know. Your physical body goes
down . . . . down . . . . down. You will find yourself in a
beautiful stream, and your Light Body will be cleansed.
You find yourself in a pool. Go up onto the beach and enter
the Lower World gates.

3. Call Huascar, the Keeper of the Underworld. Legend says
    that Huascar's brother, Altawelpa, went with the Spanish
    and helped them to conquer the people. His brother,
    Huascar, was the keeper of the medicine ways. When killed
    by his brother, Huascar was told to keep the medicine out of
    time, and the medicine is now in the Lower World. Always
    ask permission of Huascar to enter the Lower World.

Go to a boulder and call: "Huascar, Keeper of the Lower
World, come to me. I am here to find a power animal to accompany
me at this time." (Always have a clear intent when journeying.)
Always enter and leave the same way. (Do not allow anybody to
take you on a journey that does not take you out the same way.)

When I first took this journey, *I journeyed to a place my dog,
Zoe, has shown me many times, a tall cliff overlooking the ocean
with many dolphins playing. My body remained on the cliff top,
and my Light Body dove into the ocean. It was dark. The shore was
in a different ocean, and there was no meadow, but I did find the
stone. Huascar appeared as Anubis, the Egyptian God of Death
and the Underworld. All was dark. An eye appeared, and it was
like the stone creature on Star Trek, the one that laid eggs—but*

that creature had no eyes. Then it was the eye of a bear. He had
been sleeping and was not happy to be awakened. He will help
with me on this work, but now he is hibernating—it is not time. We
were called back. Come back. Come back. Come back NOW!

Learning to journey, like any other skill, takes practice. Journey
often. Always create an intention. It may be as simple as asking
questions of your power animal or of Huascar. Some sample
questions for Huascar are: What is my purpose? What can I learn
from you? What gives me strength? Why am I here now? Do you
have a message for me? Can you help me deal with _____?

Sometimes Muki may accompany you on a journey. Muki is
the keeper of the mines and ores of the Earth. He appears in many
forms. If you do not want to journey by yourself, take Muki's
hand when you dive into the Lower World. Muki will keep you
safe as you travel. Create a journal of your journeys. Go into
Luminous Awareness, ask questions, and do automatic writing for
the answers. Answers will come from the collective unconscious,
as well as your memory of the journey. You may gain additional
insights while writing.

Journey. Intent: To find a soul piece in grace.

When I went down, *it was dark. I knew I was again on the cliff*
and was more aware of going down, down, and when I reached the
shore, there was a pillar of light. Huascar flew to me and wrapped
wings around me, and a ball of light came into my heart. It was
my angry child self but happy at the same time to come back—a
softening of wanting/longing transformed into a knowingness.

Transition to the West

Before you begin the work of the West, take a few months to process what you have learned. Create your own Sacred Space at home—call it whatever you want. Upon it, place a white candle for the Santa Tierras and other colors of candles as guided by your intuition. Say: "As I light this candle, I remember to send the healed state to . . . . (name of yourself or another)." Make it a lovely place. Bring a flower to that place. Put special items in this space. Come. Sit in stillness. Practice *stillness.*

Over the next few months, allow this new awareness to inform your being. Allow your vibration to be transformed. And, as those changes are incorporated into your life, practice these steps to deepen your experience on the Shamanic Path:

1. Practice Luminous Awareness. Tinqui: I see you. Tupay: I am aware. Take: I engage.

2. Continue with the process of release. Create meaning that is empowering for you, building good medicine.

3. Assemble your reality. Really work on this as something you need in the day. As you do, you will gain clarity and the ability to see the day so you are not trapped by ego.

4. Create three solo fires in honor of the three centers. A. Honor the seed of Amaru in your belly. B. Honor Chocochinchi, the connectivity. C. Honor your vision/ framework, Apuchin. D. Then do other fires as called.

5. Connect with, and feed, your land. Start a dialog with your land. Feed it and give it gratitude. Build a Despacho for your land.

6. Both—And. Open Heart—Protection. Things we do. Be clear. Intuit. Trust. That space between "both"—"and" is Yanantin, or those two diverse things coming together.

7. Be ready, present, and available; practice beginner's mind (with the innocence of a mature person because you are experiencing it for the first time).

8. Work with the levels of engagement: energetic, mythic/ceremony, language/symbolic, and literal. Work as much as possible at the energetic and mythic levels. Think about how to create ceremony. The more you can take yourself into the mythic, the faster you can move it out with the energetic.

9. Everyday agreements:

    *   Care for yourself
    *   Care for the soul piece you received in grace
    *   Care for others
    *   Care for your indoor and outdoor space
    *   Take risks and try new things
    *   Practice trusting the process

THREE

The West: Ancestors

You will need: Three more stones. One stone should be yellow;
one stone should be black; and, one stone should be red.

Now is the time to begin the work of the West, Chocochinchi,
and Mother/Sister Jaguar. We will begin with a review of the basic
terms and definitions with which you worked in the South (Amaru,
Snake, the flow), and which will be expanded as you now journey
West.

In the work of the South, you created a Mesa. Your Mesa is a
personal altar that contains Kuyas (sacred stones) and other items
of importance to you. The Mesa is a representation of personal
transformation and healing at this stage. It now holds three stones
that hold three of your stories of past wounding. The stones
are beginning to communicate with the Apus, the Spirits of the
Mountains. The Apus say: "You no longer remember when the
stones could walk." We must now remember that, in this work,
everything is alive. As you recognize what is alive, become aware
of the synchronicities, those things you used to think were merely
coincidences. And, as you recognize all things are alive, move in
Ayni, in right relationship, with all beings. Walk with balance and
reciprocity.

Always remember the "healed state" while doing this work. If
you were in a healed/fulfilled state, what would that mean for you?

Some people are so full of their stories that it may be hard for them to heal. If you were well, what would you talk about? What would you think about? If you are in Ayni, you are probably in a healed state.

Doing things with love, balance, and with right action creates Ayni.

In working with the South, the focus was with Amaru, Serpent energy. The Serpent helps us to shed our past as a Serpent sheds its skin. It is the flow, the literal, Llankay. It is the first of the three perceptual states. In the sacral chakra area, in Amaru, lives right action. Amaru is the flow. In Amaru, everything is as it seems. Moving into the West, we work with our Ancestors, with creation energy, the energy of Jaguar.

In Jaguar, energy is often exchanged, with intent, between two people. The exchange can be positive or negative, happy or sad, but, to begin the West work, we first honor the exchanges of energy from which we were created. That exchange is called Haipay (Hi-pie). We honor the exchanges of energy with our friends and family and say "thank you." This exchange of energy can be as simple as saying "hello" or shaking hands, or as complex as meeting someone, falling in love, and creating new life. Haipay among friends is a way to exchange energy and honor the relationship with that person at the same time.

In Peru, a Shaman may take a cocoa leaf and blow his or her blessings for another into this simple gift. It is then offered to its intended recipient with a simple statement: "Welcome little dove of my heart. Will you accept this gift of love?" If the answer is "yes," the cocoa leaf is placed in the other's mouth and consumed by that person. In the Andes, cocoa leaves are used because they are readily available and help combat altitude sickness. In the United States, we often offer chocolates or other food as a gift to represent Haipay. Leaves of herb plants can also be used.

If you are working with friends, take a perfect leaf of basil or sage. Hold it sweetly in your hands and think of your friend. Bring happy memories of her or him up into your conscious mind. Think about all the ways in which you are grateful for this person's presence in your life. Then, blow all those feelings of love and gratitude into the leaf. Offer this leaf to your friend, as a blessing: "Welcome little dove of my heart. Will you accept this gift of love?" Place the leaf in your friend's mouth and let her or him be transformed by the power of your loving energy.

Another way to honor the energy between yourself and another is to create a Quintu. Quintus are usually made of three cocoa or bay leaves, each representing one of the three worlds. Basil or sage leaves, or leaves from locally growing plants, can also be used. Beautiful leaves of uniform size, all facing the same direction, stems down, placed on top of each other, glued with a little animal fat, and decorated with red and white flower petals (typically carnations), the Quintus hold your prayers. Create your Quintu and, with intent, blow blessings and prayers for another person or situation onto each. Place a red carnation leaf on each to represent Mother Earth, and add a white carnation leaf to represent the Apus. Again, blow your prayers into the Quintu and with gratitude place it upon Mother Earth.

In the West, we begin to work with Chocochinchi, the rainbow light Jaguar. Jaguar lives in our heart chakra and in the heart chakra, love also lives. Coming into the night before the new day we will see how lifelessness stalks us throughout our DNA and our ancestors. This is past life work, both karmic and ancestral. In Chocochinchi, nothing is as it seems. The work of the South and West are in the Lower World.

After the work of the West is completed, we travel to the Upper World and work in the North with Hummingbird. Working with your ancestors in the East and North, you are able to move into a healed state and travel clearly toward your personal destiny. Finally, you journey to the East, and with Eagle/Condor, you move to the source, a time of transit. In this, the third perceptual state in the area of the crown chakra, you connect with your intuition.

To begin the work of the West, go out into nature and find a "sit" spot. This is the place where you will create a Nature Painting to help you with the work you will soon begin. The process of becoming aware is tripartite:

1. Tinqui, see and be drawn to a spot;

2. Tupay, energy fields or "beings," getting closer in relationship to you; and,

3. Take: "I know it." "I embrace it." "It is my passion."

The sit spot helps you to remember where you are and how you are in relationship to something else. Place a few natural items on the ground to help you remember your spot when you return.

Next, plan a simple fire ceremony. Whenever a situation arises in which you do not know precisely how to proceed, it is time to do ceremony. Indeed, ceremony is the fastest and easiest way to move to the Shamanic way of seeing and create clarity. Ceremonies can be as elaborate as a Despacho or as simple as clearing your space. (See Chapter Eight for more information about creating Despachos and space clearing.)

To begin the work of the West, hold a simple fire ceremony. The intent for the first fire in the work of the West is to release something you need to be gone. What still is with you from the South that needs to leave now? Think about it. Find a little stick or a few flower stems. Decorate it/them with ribbon or flowers. Pray into the item. Tell it all your problems. Breathe those feelings up into your Luminous Body. Then, really blow all those emotions and feelings into your offering. Build a small fire. When the fire is ready, offer your prayers to the item and toss it into the fire. As the item burns, it transforms. All that relates to that particular issue in your life transforms in the fire. You then bring new energy into your chakras into the three centers: belly, heart, and third eye.

1. Kneel at the fire. Using your hands, bring the smoke counterclockwise into the center you are cleansing and push it out with your hands and breath back into the fire.

2. Bring the smoke into the center with your hands and hold to balance.

3. Bring the smoke in and spin the smoke clockwise to seal it in.

4. Wash yourself with smoke.

5. Wash your Mesa above the fire, circling it in the smoke seven times.

In the South, we gave up to the Earth and to the fire and to Serpent. Our Kuyas now hold the energy of those themes so we do not have to hold them anymore. The stones became changed through the rites and rituals of the fire. Once you receive rites or work with one of your teacher's stones (if appropriate), then the lineage is transferred from the Shaman's stone to yours. Your stones become part of the lineage of the people of the high Andes and that deepens the connection to the Cekes. However, if you are doing this work on your own, your stones are part of the lineage of their own birthplace. If you know the place you found your stones, connect with that place. Call on it in ceremony. Ceremony and rituals take us from the literal to the mythic. Use ritual and ceremony as much as possible to transform quickly. Know that you can make up your own ceremonies. The key is intention. The mythic changes your perception so things look different. Things feel different. And, you begin to look at things differently. Transformation and growth occur.

The work in the West is work with Shadows, with pieces of us we may not recognize. The Shadow can be many things. It may be a voice that is beautiful, just not known to you. Write in your journal before rising, and continue to make notes daily. Get into a routine with your days that include rituals. Practice being in Luminous Awareness. Stand on the Earth and be aware with all your senses: I see, hear, taste, smell, sense. Or, sit quietly and become aware of the space between your thigh and your hand. This awareness creates a state very much like hypnosis, and allows your unconscious to become more aware of "other." Indeed, until you are able to shift easily to Luminous Awareness, practice these exercises every day as you begin your daily meditation practice.

After the fire, go to bed and dream with intent. Dream to discover what you need to work with, and to release in the work of the West. As you prepare for bed, breathe deeply and set your intention to discover what still needs to be released. Repeat to yourself seven times: "I will remember my dream and know that which should be released." Place a journal and a pen next to your bed, so you can record your dream upon awakening.

In one class *I went to sleep and I dreamt of beagle puppies, dozens of them. So many beagle puppies it was hard to clean and manage them. I was angry. I was at a psychic fair with friends. The aura photographer took many pictures and gave them to me as two businesss-card-sized collages without any pictures of me. I was very angry. I went to a tuning fork exhibit and tested the A-ohm fork, and all my chakras vibrated. Then the salespeople left, and I could not buy any. I was angry. I found a lovely large (five pounds at least) peacock stone and picked it up and found it was "created," not real. I was angry. I woke up disappointed that I was not dreaming of what I needed to release. Ha! Dreams often speak in metaphor.*

I needed to work on anger. Perhaps I can release it or release the anger without knowing its cause. I set my intent to release from my energy body all anger directed at myself and at others that does not serve a purpose for my higher good. I ask forgiveness of those beings my acts have impacted and that all traces of my rage be removed also from their fields and that they be healed from my actions for all time and places and for their highest good also.

Begin your day with breathing exercises. A common exercise, to prepare for either meditation or journeying, is the "7-7-7" breath. The mind and body need to become still. This simple process also requires concentration and a shift in awareness.

1. Inhale through your nose to a count of seven. You can count to seven with one long inhale or you can "sniff" in seven times.

2. Hold your breath for a count of seven.

3. Release/Exhale through your nose to a count of seven. Again, you can exhale in a long breath or "sniff" your breath out.

4. Hold for a count of seven.

5. Repeat a total of seven times.

The goal is for each count of seven to be equal. That may not happen until breath five or six! Some days, the mind does not want to slow down.

The 7-7-7 breathing process puts your mind in a state where its perception can change and open. The world changes when you change your perception. The greatest and quickest shifts you can make are at the energetic level. The hardest place to shift is at the literal level. Bringing light into the body and sealing it also allows your perception to heal and shift. At the mythic level, the quality of how you walk in the world, the pattern of Victim/Perpetrator/Rescuer can change. "I walk with joy." "I embrace that which comes to me." These affirmations come at a different level. Once cleared energetically, the affirmations can help make faster, literal changes.

The end result of this Mesa work is for you to be empowered. Your Mesa moves from that of the "wounded healer" to the "collective." You are then in munay. In munay, you are in the natural order of reciprocity (*i.e.*, the going in, and out; feeding/being fed; the love the lion feels for the antelope before taking it down; right relationship; unconditional cosmic love). Nothing tracks Jaguar for food, so she lives fearlessly. As Jaguar, let go of the fear that has come to you through your ancestors and your karma. Fear causes us to live as though death stalks us. In this work, we say there is no enemy in this world or the next. We no longer project; no longer argue about who we are. If someone says something about you, you can say, "that is his or her projection." You need not accept that projection as yourself.

We will learn how not to engage when provoked; how to pick battles; how not to react, but, instead, how to shift, be present, and not be ruled by the need to be right. We will discuss symbols of empowerment. We will look at ancestral DNA and our karmic lineage, and we will release some of the predetermined debt that we carry. We will track what we need to help ourselves and help others. What has happened in this time, in this life, as well as that stored by your ancestors in this body, will go into your stones.

In the work of the South, three themes of your woundedness were cleared from your Luminous Body. The energy was transformed and moved into the stones. Ceremony transformed the stones into Kuyas. They are now the stones of a Shaman and carry the lineage of their origin and perhaps that of the high Andes, as well.

To help heal others on this path or to work on other themes and issues, you can use your Kuyas to clear the Luminous Body and shift at the energetic level. Ceremony then moves those issues at the mythic level, and you no longer need to carry those stories. When you have an issue, a story, that needs to be released, choose a stone that "speaks" to you or feels good in your hand. Talk your story (or stories) into the stone. Blow those stories in. Set the stone into a Nature Painting for two to three days to let nature work with that energy. Every day go out two or three times and talk with the stone. Then, holding the stone, check to see what chakra holds those stories. Which is spinning counter clockwise, discharging that story into your field? Work with the lowest chakra and one of your Kuyas to clear that issue. When the chakra is no longer discharging energy, clear your Kuya with Florida Water.

If you have quite a few issues with which you need to work, you may not want to create a Kuya for each issue. Re-using a stone that has already transformed from the literal level (of being a stone), to the mythic level (of hearing your stories and being in a Nature Painting), to the energetic level (by being smudged in fire ceremony) is perfectly okay, too. The stones are capable of holding thousands of stories of our life's wounding and are not harmed when the fire takes those issues to the energetic level numerous times.

To help others to release their issues energetically, see the Illumination process in Chapter Nine. Be aware that, when you do this work to help others heal, you may accidentally take on "stuff" that is not yours. To prevent this, always work in Sacred Space. Open your Wiracocha with the intent that your Luminous Body will remain clear. Ask that the Earth, the fire, and the stones take this "stuff." The power in your stones is the power of a wounded healer's Mesa. This power, created by you in the process of taking your issues to the energetic level, allows your Luminous Body to remain clear.

Soul Retrieval

Sometimes things happen to us, and we want to hide. Some of these things are truly horrific, and the memory of these events is traumatic. Some of these happened in the past, or have happened in many different lifetimes, creating a pattern in our Luminous Body. Some of these events are less physically traumatic, but emotionally embarrassing or hurtful. All of these events may create soul loss. A little piece of us hides to be safe, got lost, or has gone into hiding. That piece may be waiting to be called home. The pieces stay hidden until we look for them.

Although the Shamanic healing technique of soul retrieval is beyond the scope of this book, talented practitioners are available around the world to assist you with this process. The Shaman will journey deep into your Lower World and search for parts of you in hiding. He or she will go to the original source of your wounding, be it in this lifetime or a past life, and ask for a gift to heal the you of now. We need to bring all of the soul pieces that are in grace back to ourselves to heal. Pachamama says: "I need my children to come home. Come home." Set your intention to journey with Muki, or your spirit guide, to find a lost part of yourself. Know that whatever it is that happened, you survived and are safe in the now. Be welcoming, assuring, and loving as you recover little bits of yourself through the journey. When you come back, create a ceremony to remember the Earth and to ask the Earth to hold you. With ceremony, the Earth remembers you. When that happens, you can come home. Welcome the little bits of yourself back with ceremony and love.

Exercise. Journey to the Lower World for another person with the purpose of finding an anima, a soul piece or fragment ready to come back. When you find the piece gather it up and put it in a chakra—usually the heart or the crown but do not get stuck there in case something else feels right. Intuit where it needs to be. The anima is that which travels while you journey. Ask for those pieces in grace ready to come back to come, come, come. Call on their anima. Really invite it/them back. Gather the pieces that you find in grace. Blow them into the body where they belong. Blow. Fold the person's hands over that center. Let it rest. Draw a Chakana (an Andean, or equal-armed cross) under their hands. Give the person some time to assimilate this new piece. Have them ask that piece what to do to keep it safe again.

Transformation

Be aware of which part of you is engaging with others: energetic, mythic, symbolic, literal? In the West work, if we own all of "who" we are, we no longer cast a Shadow and we no longer project those aspects we have disowned onto others. Become aware of what you project and what you are receiving from others. Remember: we have no enemies in this world or the next. We step beyond our adversarial role and help to shift the world. When we become the healed state, we do not have to do a lot in order to remain balanced and centered. We are able to recognize the various states of awareness and shift to the state that best suits what we are doing. For example, if you are standing in a long line at airport security, it is best to view the process through the eyes of Amaru or Apuchin. Seeing the line as it is, and without emotion, is a much better way of coping than moving into the churned up state of Chocochinchi.

Go beyond death (the little-by-little deaths leaving you more lifeless than alive) so death no longer stalks you. Release the life experiences that transform you—mulch them—so the bad, as well as the good, in those experiences can then be transformed and nourish your life. Shed the fear all at one time, and encounter the love that is part of the collective. Practice non-engagement. Pick your battles carefully. No longer bring to you that which you fear most. Release fear.

The Apus say: "Go to the effect you want, not the reactivity that causes it. Do not be ruled by a need to be right." Be aware of the archetypes and of the fact that being a Victim/Perpetrator/Rescuer disempowers you. Violence is created by disempowerment and rage. Release your ancestral, genetic, and karmic lineage. You will be able to attract your destiny, instead of fear-driven junk that is in the way. Clear the way to your becoming and change the way death stalks those in your genetic lineage. Voluntarily release the predetermined death planned for you. Shed the life selected for you, and step into the life that you know is your essence. You will become a Caretaker of the Earth.

Journey. Intent: To meet Huascar and a power animal, and ask what is it I need to know before I begin the work of the West? What do I need to know? If you see a picture of something or are given a gift, usually it is not in the literal and you may need to ask, what is the meaning?

In one of my journeys, *on the rock Zoe showed me, my spirit body exited as a large black bird. I dove into the water and went down, down. Floating in the water, I was I but not I—female—then male and naked. I came out onto the pool and came to the rock. I was not aware of Huascar but of my totem animal, Giraffe, and his child. They showed me a large rock with me sitting there or lying on it meditating. I spent some time doing this. I know where to go, Giraffe said. I was called back. I dove again into the pool, the stream, but as I came back out of the Earth through the ocean, I was a large blue bird and I flew back into my body. Note to self: ask for further understanding in dreamtime.*

Exercise. A method of cleansing the physical and spirit body is with candles. Use a white candle and a candle of the appropriate color palate for the day you are doing the cleansing. The colors have a relationship to spirit and spirit to power. Or, you can track what color that you need or your client needs and trust in that intuition. When cleansing, always use white first and then use the color of the day for a little deeper work.

Monday—Lunes—Moon—White

Tuesday—Martes—Mars—Red

Wednesday—Miercoles—Mercury—Violet/Purple

Thursday—Hueves—Jupiter—Blue

Friday—Viernes—Venus—Green

Saturday—Sabado—Saturn—Black. NEVER use black candles because they are associated with the "dark side." Do not do this exercise on Saturday.

Sunday—Domingo—Sun—Yellow/Gold

Know that when you light a candle or wear the color of the day, Spirit responds and is honored you recognized it! The candle cleansing is a cleaning with fire. You roll the dense energy out of the body and into the candle.

1. Open your Wiracocha over yourself and your client, creating double Sacred Space.

2. Roll the candle(s) all over the body, down the head, over every inch of the whole body.

3. Take a piece of white paper and roll the candle in it, leaving the flame end out. Take it far from where you are and light it. As you light it say: "It ends here. It ends here. It ends here." Light the candle and leave it.

After my journey to find out what more I needed to know before beginning the work of the West, I asked for help in my dream. There, I saw *golden eagles everywhere. Circles of women taking away pain, moving from jealousy to love, moving into a new and peaceful place. Doing lots of laundry. Clarity of clearing. A small animal that could not live with me went to a new home, but I could access it with my member card until 2013. Darkness. Tunnels. Searching. Lots of searching and not finding. Lots of waking and not sleeping. Lots of being up and wishing for more.* Dreams often speak in metaphor and metaphor is not something I have ever been "good" at. Golden eagles represent the sun. Groups of women, acting as healers. Cleaning clothes. Clarity. Cleaning. Dreamtime messages I could not interpret. If this happens to you, write what you remember anyway. Often, they become clearer over time, and you can re-read them a few months later and have a grand "a-ha!" moment.

Remember that harmony does not mean being in perfect balance. Balance is a dualistic thing of trying to make things the same. The Andean people prefer the complement of differences and to preserve the individuality of the two entities.

Pay attention to projections. Recognize what you are projecting and what projections you are accepting. Projections help to build that ego structure of "who am I?" As adults, we can ease up. We often take on projections of family, friends, colleagues, etc. Keep what serves you, and then loosen up, learn to embrace life, and remember who you really are. Now, there are <u>choices</u>.

In the work of the West, we begin to work with three types of Cekes:

1. Kayao (kie-a-o). This Ceke is between the personal and everything else. There is a cause, then an effect. Kayao is limited to your experience. Kayao is expressed in the first center of exchange, in the belly. First, this happens; then, that happens. First, on the edge of the land. you see a little leaf on a tree. Then you notice a little stream going to the river. First, you see your mother. Then, you eat dinner. This is the Ceke of you and your personal connections.

2. Payan (pie-yawn). This Ceke is still limited by space and time but is broader. For example, the Mississippi River is a place and time, but it is joined to a much broader aspect of time and place in that as "river," it has existed in other times and other expressions of "place." Payan is "an expansion of the connection"—a broader Ceke connection.

3. Kollana (ko-yan-a). These are Cekes that go beyond time and space, beyond light, timeless. The Cekes of the primary relationship to Source/Creation, *i.e.*, the Milky Way.

Be aware of all kinds of Cekes, all those connections you have with places, people, animals, plants, etc. First, remember your own Kayao Cekes. See your connection as a thread or line attached from you to the other and from the others to you. Broaden that vision to your Payan Cekes. See how you, and your ancestors, may be connected to a place. See how that place changes over linear time. See the fluidity in time and place, and how your connection may enhance your awareness of a place in the now. From that place of timeless connection, see your connection to Kollana Cekes. Move into the universe, into other galaxies, and become aware of all the connections. Go to a connection of the creative force available when going out deeper and further. Expand your Cekes to the ancient force within us. Cekes are like a spider's web. So much is interconnected, but all the lines lead to the center and from there, back to you.

Exercise. This exercise is an awareness method to take you to your mythic level. The cards take you out of the literal and help you get to where you need to go faster. Using any tarot deck, draw three cards and write a story about what you see in the pictures. The first card allows you to begin the story very traditionally. Start with the words "Once upon a time . . . ." The second card will tell you the middle of the story, what happened next. The third card shows you the end of the story. This exercise can be done alone or in groups of three, each person drawing a card. The group uses the same cards to tell the story. With your story, write down the things you liked most about the main character. Write down the things you did not like. Then read your story aloud. Read it aloud again. The third time you read aloud, read your story in the first person. Where is the energy? What jumps out at you as you make the shift to the "I"? Listen at a deep level. Be a witness. Look for a message in your story.

For example, in this exercise, one time my group used:
(1) The Hierophant, (2) Justice, and (3) The Star. *I looked carefully at the cards, and began: "Once upon a time, a wealthy man sat upon a throne. Strong animals that loved him surrounded him and his heart glowed golden in his chest. A great light poured from his heart to those surrounding him. A happy God smiled down upon this wealthy man, and an Egyptian Goddess grew between his legs, sending the tendrils of her gown into the Earth. All of the animals with the man were happy and contented in this life but one on the man's right side. An argument ensued between the light and joy and the dark and grim. A King, yielding a golden sword, was called upon to determine the fate of the wealthy man, his animals, and his God. A balanced scale in one hand, the King determines for all what is good and just. In this justice, the world shifted. The world glowed. The animals became crystals of light energy supporting the Earth. The Goddess became a beautiful and flexible maiden supporting the scales of light justice and the now-crystalline sword. The scales of light floated over the maiden. Through her dance, the Earth became round and full and all beings danced and sang and were healed. All beings were in their proscribed place, ready to move into their perfect state of being and purpose. The end.*

I liked that the King had many friends and loved animals and his heart glowed. I liked that he was loved by animals and surrounded by them. I liked that a happy God smiled down on him. I did not like that the King worried about staying wealthy and worried when others did not like him. I did not like that he seemed to be suppressing his feminine side. Moral: Justice is needed to transform to the healed state.

Exercise. Find a place on your land to do a Nature Painting. Put some kind of perimeter around it with sticks and flowers. Remember that as you work with Spirit and the Nature Painting shifts, you shift. Open Sacred Space around your painting.

Sit quietly and begin to rattle. Journey to the Lower World, and ask Huascar or a power animal you meet there to help you. Ask: "What shadows do I need to take a look at for myself?" In my journey, "*Hawk flew over. Horse came and left. Owl came. Huascar was a light being; he took my hand, and Owl stayed on my shoulder. I need to identify and release the blocks on my heart. This will heal my body physically, as well as allow the deeper communication with animals and nature I desire. Salmon came; his lips moved, but I could not understand the words. I could not read Salmon's lips. I was called back.*

Exercise. Go to your Nature Painting. Sit with your three stones. In this work, it is important that one stone is yellow, one stone is red, and one stone is black. Make a list of the ancestors of whom you are aware and who have had an influence on your life. It is easier if these are people who are no longer alive but who you knew in this life. If you were adopted or raised by people not blood relations, choose three of your adoptive family relations and, with intent, transform them into your blood relations. Let that blood relation play the role of the adopted person in your life. You want to work with the DNA your blood relations provided you.

Choose three blood relations. Put some thought into why you are choosing them. How did they affect your life? What lessons did you learn from them? We will elevate all ancestors, "good and bad," to the altar. We will take them out of the DNA strands and place them into the stones. Make sure both of your bloodlines are represented. You will either have two ancestors from your father's side of the family and one from your mother's side, or vice versa. If you can, have a partner to work as a witness. If you are working with a partner, you will find that partners are often able to ask questions that will deepen your answers. If no one is available to help, write as fully as you can in your journal. Working with one ancestor, and one stone, at a time:

1. Write the ancestor's full name, relationship to you, and how this ancestor influenced you on a piece of paper. Choose a stone and write down the color of the stone that represents this ancestor.

2. You are going to tell your partner, or your journal, why you chose that ancestor. Then, you will blow this information into one of the stones. Open Sacred Space as you journal, or allow your partner to hold you in Sacred Space, and answer the following questions:

   • Tell me about the ancestor and how they affected your life?

   • How did that ancestor die? Or how might they be dying of lifelessness now?

   • What did you learn from that relationship?

   • How is the theme of the way they died present in your life now? Is it?

- How does their life live within you now?

- Was there something that drained their life force?

- What is the challenge they left with you?

- What is the gift? How do you want to remember them?

- What was incomplete in their life that they left for you to complete?

- Were there unfulfilled dreams, hopes, and challenges?

As you talk about your ancestors, blow this story into the stone. After you finish talking about one ancestor, place it in your Nature Painting with the piece of paper naming that ancestor.

3. Repeat with all three stones.

Leave the East door of your painting open. East is the direction of the Pacharinas, that which sprints forth in the new day. An opening in the circle allows new energy to flow into the painting. It also allows stuck or stagnant energy to flow out. Know that you do not have to hold these stories anymore. They are just stories. Give them to the West. Give them to the setting sun. These stories are the ending of some old Pachas/stuff you have been holding. You are beginning a new Pacha, with new stories. Giving the stories up to the stones, to the Kuyas, to the Earth, to the elements, and to the Universe allows a shift. And, as something shifts in the Nature Painting, so also do you shift.

4. Let the stones rest overnight.

In the morning, go again to your painting. Working alone, or with a partner, hold each stone one at a time. Ask which chakra is holding the energy of that ancestor in your Luminous Field. Or, ask your partner to hold the stone in his/her left hand and check which of your chakras is affected by that energy. The lowest one going counter clockwise is holding the energy of that ancestor's DNA. Add that to your notes about that ancestor. Work with the stones (and clearing that chakra) will continue later.

Death and Rebirth

Now, we work on dying to a new beginning. To what do you want to die? What do you want to let go of in yourself, let die in yourself, so you are no longer stalked by lifelessness? What do you need to let go of forever? Let go of things that no longer serve you. Write them in your journal. Take your written words to the fire and release these from your energy body. Think about this transformation. And then, write your own eulogy. This should not be the list of facts and relatives printed in the newspaper to announce a transition. Your eulogy does not need to be what you do professionally per se either. Write down how you *want* to be remembered. If you are working with a group, write it clearly enough so that someone else can read it.

My eulogy went something like this: *Born in the year of the Serpent with the guidance of the crab and the healing vibration of the number 9, Lorie Allen departed her body, leaving a legacy of stories, music, and joy. When she stopped trying to "fix" everyone and everything, Lorie's life filled with dogs, horses, birds, other wild animals, fish, plants, stones, and trees who shared stories with her, that she shared with us. Lorie was a true and much loved "nut," who lived and walked in joy. As her spirit moves to the next spoke of the wheel, may she continue her dance into love and fulfillment. She goes now to the Source, surrounded by the lights of those she loved and who loved her who went before, transformed to the Stones where she began.*

Exercise. At this point in a Shamanic class, students experience the "mini-death" and are reborn. This exercise may only be done under the supervision and guidance of a Shamanic practitioner with extensive experience in these rites, and I will not write about them here. However, when doing this work on your own, it is important to recognize your own death in order to be reborn without your ancestor's baggage. To do that, open Sacred Space. Open your Wiracocha. If you are alone, read your eulogy out loud. Rattle and take five to ten minutes to think about your life and the influence your ancestors have had upon that life. If you are in a group, hold a brief "funeral" ceremony. Sit quietly in the center of your group while someone else: (1) reads the eulogy, (2) talks about your life (as friends and family would at a funeral), and (3) says a prayer. Feel a little bit what it is like to die and to be reborn. Close the Wiracocha.

In the "little death" rites, the Luminous Body, as well as the physical, actually experience death in the literal sense. The breath stops (or seems to stop). The light is exquisite. Visions come and go very quickly. The Luminous Body is only hovering above the physical for a minute. It seems much longer. It takes five to ten minutes to come back and be again aware of the physical. After this experience, there is no reason to fear death. Death no longer stalks you and no longer awakens fear.

When you meditate, do so in a darkened room without candles. Sit quietly and open your Wiracocha three times. Go into Luminous Awareness and feel the edges of your light body. Call on the Apus. Ask them to be present. Ask for them by name: Apus Ausangate, Salcantay, Veronica, Pachatusan, Mama Simuna, Huaca Wilka, Machu Picchu, Huaynu Picchu, Manuel Pinto, and Yanantin. And, in North America, also call Apus Everest, Shasta, Hood, and Rainier. Try and sit for a period of time each day and ask the Apus to come. Feel the light cloak that carries you; feel that it is intact. You access the world through the assemblage point in your Luminous Body. There is a donut-hole shape in the Luminous Body through which we access the world. Information comes in at different places on different people. Look for a place that feels different, like a little window in your field. This is your assemblage point. Often it is close to your sacral chakra. Find it and where it informs your body. It can be a different place at different times. When you find it, use this point to learn to shift perceptual states. Your neurological pathways can change through awareness, choice, and practice. The quickest changes take place at the energetic, so a new way of walking in the world, exhibited by behavioral changes, takes place.

You can view your Wiracocha as an expansion of your eighth chakra. Remember your belly, the lower Tan Tien, that area of Amaru, the Lower World. This is the organizing principle of the flow of all this. It is the fluidity, the flow of all through your whole life. In the East—newness—dawn—all springs ever coming from the Pacharinas. Sometimes the flow is stopped. The archetype here is Serpent. It is as it is, literal and without judgment. The perceptual state here is to care for the physical. Kundalini energy keeps you connected with Yachay, the area of right action.

In your heart chakra, there is connectivity and the feeling that nothing is as it seems. This is the world of emotion and the world of the rainbow light Jaguar. In the heart is the center of munay, the center of love. For what things do you feel an affinity? What are you beginning to learn?

In right love/right relationship you have connectivity without actually being reactive to a situation. What helps with this aspect of being is Apuchin. With the help of the third eye, detaching as an Eagle/Condor, you can see a situation in its entirety and be connected without reacting.

Serpent. Literal. It is as it is. Attention to detail. No judgment. Western medicine is all in Serpent. Jaguar. Symbolic. Nothing is as it seems to be. It is daytime dreaming. It is projection. Eagle. Mythic. Seeing how everything is in relation to everything else. Poof. Clear. Let it go. Completely surrender. Now, completely at the energetic level, give to Spirit. Give it up. It is done.

Really practice these. Be aware: In which center am I? How am I viewing the world? Who is seeing? When you change perceptual states, it can shift what other people perceive and change the energy of the space, as well. In healing, go to Eagle/Condor or go to the level above that which your client is currently experiencing. This helps to raise the client's vibration, as well.

Serpent—as it is—physical—fluidity
Jaguar—nothing is at it seems—mythic—connectivity
Eagle—get a bigger picture—almost energetic—framework of the whole deal
Above the eighth chakra to Spirit—the energetic
Poof—it is gone

Take this awareness of transformation back to your stones. Become aware of the Ceke lines that connect them. Honor your land, take the honoring and the core connection you have, and connect your Ceke lines as you travel. Honor the Earth there. One way to honor is by recognition. You can enhance the recognition with your prayers into a Quintu using the blessing: "I honor you." Carry small gifts in your Mesa to use as offerings to the Earth and to help you to remember.

Go and sit with your Nature Painting. Look for any changes or shifts in the painting since you were last there.

I noticed only small things as I went back to my painting: *Ah! There is an opening in the southeast that was not there before. Ants are there! A fly landed on my arm, but I brushed her away forgetting to accept her healing. Robin greeted me on the path, and birds now sing all around. Now a small green spider on a blade of grass is in the center.*

Remove the stones from the painting.

Remember the drama triangle; when you stay in a Jaguar state you get caught in the Victim/Perpetrator/Rescuer cycle. The Perpetrator is the one most often in Shadow for someone. As a result of our actions, someone becomes a Victim. The Rescuer thinks, if we help others enough, we can get what we need. You do not want to be caught here either. We change places in the triangle to keep this going, and in most families of origin, this is a perceptual cycle. By doing this work, we learn to own being victim or perpetrator. When we recognize our role, then we can get out of the cycle. The projections are the illusions of the Jaguar state. Do not accept the stuff of others, and do not project your own. You have to flip out of the triangle to be a whole person. Any time you have an upset (any kind of upset small or large), take the opportunity to shape shift and take a look. Make a Despacho if need be. Make an offering and have a fire ceremony. By bringing to light the possibilities, you can step back and take a new look.

Exercise. Find three sticks. Use the Lineage Stone you created, or a stone from a Shaman's Mesa, and one of your new stones. Remember which chakra held the energy of each ancestor. Remember which stone held that energy: red, black, or yellow. You are going to track heaviness or emotional density in the Luminous Field from each level of awareness (Amaru, Chocochinchi, Apuchin). How do you see this person walking in this world? Remember the three ways of knowing the world: visual, auditory, and kinesthetic. We can then see where the filaments of light are connected to our DNA through our ancestors. Then we will unwind them and put them in the fire tonight. When the field has density, what comes in and goes out is not clear. The density is cleared from the Luminous Body and moves to the stones and sticks.

When the sticks go to the fire, the energy clears energetically, transforming you at the mythic level.

Exercise. If you are working alone, you will not be able to track how your body holds the energy of each ancestor at the visual, auditory, and kinesthetic levels. However, you will be able to unwind this energy from your Luminous Body and transform it in the fire. Remove all jewelry, watches, earrings, rings, etc. Open your Wiracocha. Take a stone. Remember to which ancestor it corresponds. The stone holds the ancestor who has influenced your life. Now that you have been reset, you have changed. Blow into that stone any material left that no longer serves you. Bring it up energetically, and while it is there, blow it THREE times into the stone. Breathe gently and slowly to hold the energy of that ancestor. Using your pendulum, check your chakras to find the chakra to which that ancestor belongs. If the chakra spins clockwise, that is not it. A chakra spinning counterclockwise is holding that ancestor's imprint. The lowest chakra spinning counterclockwise is primary. Work on clearing the lowest and others come into balance. Using your Lineage Stone, and each of your ancestor stones one at a time, hold the two stones with a little stick in between them. Do the 7-7-7 breath and, while holding your breath, unwind the lowest chakra discharging counterclockwise into the stick. Then, unwind the energy all over the body as you are guided to do. Unwind only while holding the breath. The Lineage Stone helps move the energy from the chakra and your Luminous Body into the stick and into the ancestor's stone. The energy of that ancestor goes through the stones into the stick. Repeat with all three stones, using a new stick each time. Clear your Lineage Stone with Florida Water between each use, also.

Exercise. This exercise may not be done alone. Working in groups of four: Person A works with their stones and sticks; Person B checks chakras and rattles; Persons C and D sit close together and track where the energy is moving and shifting.

Person C-D: Open Wiracocha over persons A and B.

Person A. Remove all jewelry, watches, earrings, rings, etc. Take a stone. Remember to which ancestor it corresponds. The stone holds the ancestor who has influenced your life. Now that you have been reset, you have changed. Blow into that stone any material left that no longer serves you. Bring it up energetically, and while it is there, <u>blow</u> it THREE times into the stone. Give the stone to Person B. Breathe gently and slowly to hold the energy of that ancestor. Person B then rechecks the chakras to find the chakra to which that ancestor belongs. If the chakras pins clockwise, that is not it. A counterclockwise chakra is discharging. The lowest spinning that way is primary. Work on clearing the lowest and others come into balance. Persons C and D, track Person A's energy field at the three levels of awareness: Serpent, Jaguar, and Eagle. How does Person A look with this ancestor in her body? Person B rattles and records. The goal here is to get a map of how the person works in their body. Do this with each of the three stones. As persons C and D track, remember there is no interpretation or analysis, just what is.

Person A holds a stone, a stick, and a Lineage or Shaman's stone. Others now hold the four directions as Person A stands in the center and does the 7-7-7 breath, the little death breath. One person counts aloud: inhale 7, hold 7, exhale 7, and hold 7.

Person A unwinds the chakras only while holding the breath. Start unwinding at the chakra that held the energy of that ancestor and then go to other places on the body and unwind all areas until the process is intuitively complete. The goal is to pull out those energies, those strands of DNA, which do not belong. The energy will be held in the sticks and released to the fire. You will work with all three stones and a separate stick for each.

When this process is complete (either individually or as a group), go to the fire and hold an ancestral fire ceremony. <u>As you go out of the DNA lineage, you will come into the wider lineage of the Earthkeepers</u>! As you work with issues in your life, use the perceptual states of awareness to "Poof" the issue to spirit. "Give" it up; it is done.

This is heart work. Your heart lineage connects with the luminous warrior who practices peace and dares to speak her truth. In the heart work, remember:

1. Do not collude with consensual reality. It takes a high level of integrity not to agree with what everyone else is doing, or to make assumptions. You need to be compromising to meet people's needs. Be motivated by the powerful state of ethics, not the belief systems of others.

2. Practice non-engagement. Select your battles carefully. Try not to be reactive but to practice those perceptive states of Eagle/Condor-Jaguar-Serpent. Is this battle worth my energy?

3. There are no back doors. You may need to burn some bridges. If you tend to hold on to unhealthy connections, remember that warriors burn bridges and do not need to cross that bridge again! Do not create anything that keeps you from being engaged in the present. Have no doubt. Have trust in Spirit and fully step into your life.

4. Be totally negotiable and completely uncompromising. Do not get stuck in defending your position. Do not compromise the essence or core of yourself or your vision. Come to the core of who you <u>are</u>.

5. When you change the concept of what you are doing—what you are—perceptions shift. Stay in your *core*.

Transition to the North

The Pampamesayoq are a line of medicine men and women who exist outside of linear time and have developed a relationship as stewards of life. You, too, can develop a relationship of stewardship of life. Have fire ceremonies to honor the lineage to begin the relationship.

Your stones are now more than stones. They are Kuyas, charged stones. The stones carry all the remembrances of the places from which it came, as well as your stories and those of your ancestors. Do a fire ceremony for each Kuya. If needed, do the 7-7-7 breath and, when holding each stone, ask for release using a stick and then put it to the fire.

The final journey before transiting to the North is to your past lives. Each of us has a garden in the Lower World. In our garden, we are safe and memories of past experiences can be found there. Next plan to journey to the garden. First, you will journey to a life of pain; then to a life you wasted; and, finally, to a life of joy. Instructions for the journey are followed by my journey in italics, as an example.

Journey to the Garden. Set your intention to journey to the garden, going in and out the same way, without expectations. Holding each stone, journey first with the black stone to a life of pain.

Into the past; only roots instead of feet; appeared to be a tree—then life in the tree; alone; alone; burning; alone; hanging; burning black; then held by angels; back to the pool of white sand and held by Jaguar.

Journey with your red stone to a life wasted.

A small child sitting on a rock swinging her feet. Great gift of knowing and seeing. Orphaned; lived in a huge house. Raised by people wanting her money. She used that money to destroy and kill the beauty she left behind as a child. Older she was shrouded; placed alive in a catacomb. But when I held her she transformed into a beautiful young woman. Hello, little one. I know, and all is forgiven. All is well.

Journey with your yellow stone to a life of joy.

A healer with the gift of listening, understanding, and using plants in ways that healed and made whole. A life in a deep woods with a plain and mountains in the distance. A woman. A bearded and cloaked man with feathers on his cloak. A bard. A teacher. A woman surrounded by light and angels at death. Into the light; then rising up as a feathered being. Here now.

Run your fingers up the back of your neck and as your spine attaches to your head there are two small indentations. These are "deepening" points that can be held to help you release stuck energy. These points are also places where, while meditating or journeying or in the dreamtime, information from the Universe can enter. Allow information to flow, and use your intuition to help you interpret this information and act upon it in Ayni.

Walk in your yard or a nearby park. Sense where the energy of your land is "oldest." Feel where the "ancestors" of the land reside. This may be an old tree, a boulder, a pond, or just a sense you get in one place. You may even sense this kind of space in your house or apartment. Near this space, create an ancestral altar. If the ancestral place is a tree, ask her what she wants—feed her—place a gift in her bark (*e.g.*, unworn or leftover jewelry or a small crystal). She will shimmer. Remember agreements made in the South for yourself and others, both indoors and outdoors. Clear out the literal. Expand by taking risks.

You need not "give up" modern amenities to follow this path. The Apus said we should use our technology. However, use Quintus in gratitude for lessons learned. Release each ancestor and release the past lives. Create your own ceremony and transform to the sacred.

FOUR

The North: Now

You will need: Three very beautiful stones.

Step into <u>now</u>.

Timelessness. Embrace being in the <u>now</u>. No longer allow the past to inform who you are. If there is still a story holding you, do a ceremony, go to your Mesa, let go of the secret and heal. Every moment, every piece of <u>now</u>, is sacred. Embrace the <u>now</u>.

Practice invisibility. When you no longer react to something but are in the <u>now</u>, you no longer attach and no longer leave footprints in the snow. If "it" shows up in you, there is an affinity for that thing. Realize that you need to work on that issue. That is, if something bothers you in others, you have an affinity and it may be in you. Work on it! If you spot "it," you've got "it." Look for those affinities, those things that aggravate you. Work with them, and then let them go.

What tools do you have for transformation? They are already many: fire; the Despacho; the Nature Painting; journeying; smudging with sage/incense; and candle clearing. Go to the sacredness of ceremony.

The wheel now becomes a medicine path. We do not have to process stuff emotionally or in our bodies. We have pulled off the stories, and can now process things more mythically and symbolically. We understand our nature and are be-coming more of who we really are. The journey now becomes a spiritual path. We are no longer under the influence of cause and effect, and can engage our life from a different place. Step back. Get out of the rescuer mode. You are no longer your old stories. You <u>now</u> experience the joy of being with all that is.

Now is the time to remember the journey of the ancient feminine, Pachamama. Now is the time to remember who we are. When we remember, we can embody our full purpose and bring this current feminine of the now back to the Earth to remember Pachamama at *this* time. Women hold the ancient fire. Santa Tierras are the feminine spirits of the land. They hold and nurture Pachamama. There are two types of Santa Tierras who live at the center of the Earth, and they hold the fire in two parts: (1) warming, supporting, and cooking; and (2) destructive, explosive, and tearing things asunder. In coming back to the ancient feminine that *is us*, it is time now for deconstruction. However, the Santa Tierras are now having a difficult time holding the energy of the land. The cities push against them, and the low vibration caused by much of man's work on the planet makes it very hard for them. The cities expand onto the land creating much distress for the Santa Tierras. Now, they, too, will be remembered and welcomed at our fires by name:

- Welcome Santa Tierra Plazeleta ley Bolyn, who holds the land by a cathedral of the same name.

- Welcome Santa Warmi, who holds the energy of the big cathedral on the major square in Cusco. There she takes the tears of those who come to her and transforms them into pearls.

95

- Welcome Killia Wasi, who holds space at the House of the Moon at Huayna Picchu.

- Welcome Pancha Kollya, who holds the Inka's last stronghold at Wilka Bamba.

- Welcome all the "over lighting Devas," the spirits of nature that nourish all that is on the Earth, of our land.

In the work of the South and the West, much came apart. In the resting time between those directions, integration and healing took place. After that deconstruction is revolution via rebirth and renewal. It is now time to be as clear as possible so what we put out, and what returns to us, is also clear and very positive. It is a time that thoughts and actions result in rapid manifestation. Things are now moving very fast. It is time to be open to opportunity, to really move along with the flow. It is time to live in that flow, a space more out of time. With this speed up of time, it is time to focus more on your physical body and how to set boundaries. Setting boundaries and self-care are now more important than ever. How are you caring for yourself? Do you need to do more? What? How are you caring for your space? How are you doing taking risks? Do you trust the process?

Remember, you only get out what you put in. Now the work is shifting and becoming part of everyday life. By recognizing this shift, the ordinary becomes exquisite. The ordinary is enough. We now have all we need. Being forgiving of yourself and shifting perceptual states allow you to see in Luminous Awareness more of the time. By shifting perceptual states and being in Luminous

Awareness, you can detach from the drama around you and can live and act with a high level of awareness. Use the gifts of the Santa Tierras, and *trust,* and access pure *intuition*. Do this with gratitude. Really live in gratitude. Have the discipline to do that every day. Language is important. Watch what you are saying. What you say creates energy, and you want only positive energy. You can still be compassionate, caring, and *present* for others, but you no longer have to take on other's stuff as your own. Be aware. Stay in the now.

The Santa Tierras have given us Seven Rays of Light to work with this new process:

- Physical

- Strength

- Emotion/Love

- Concrete Mind

- Pure Mind

- Intuition

- Voluntant—the apex of the pyramid. It is said that there is a crystal pyramid under the plaza at Machu Picchu. It is said that when the Machu Picchu pyramid is activated, all the other pyramids on Earth will be activated.

In the North, we will work with invisibility, mastery of time, and sacredness. Here, one receives the Wisdom Keeper rites of the high Andes, bringing us to a higher vibrational level and drawing into our life higher vibrational relationships. This is Earth work. When the North is complete, the work of the East allows you to take this work out into the world.

The Apus, mountain spirits in Peru and elsewhere, work with us in this direction. The Apus provide the structure of the highest vibrations, the building blocks so to speak. Apu Ausangate creates a higher vibration in humans, as well as in animals, other beings, and places on Earth. Apu Salcantay helps us work with our Mesa and Mesa creation. Apu Pacha Tucson holds the balance, the axis of the world at this time. And, in 2012, Apu Everest, in North America, has joined the work, as have Apu Mt. Rainier and Apu Mt. Shasta. In North America, people need the land-based knowledge that we forgot long ago. In South America, there is a need for technology. Soon, North and South America will be able to "fly together." The Eagle of North America and the Condor of South America will learn to fly together. The vibration of the Earth and all her beings will rise.

To begin the work of now, create a fire ceremony to release anything still left of the West. To begin, think again of your life list and those who taught you. People who were your teachers in school, but also friends and family who helped you learn and helped shape who you are now, will be honored and released. Make a list of your teachers, everyone who helped in allowing you to be who you are at this point. They may not all be people. Take some time with this project. And at the end of the list, add a line "for all those who helped inform me and are not named." Then go into nature and find a lovely small stick or some other natural item of beauty to place in the fire. Wrap your list around your offering and create a fire ceremony honoring the work of the South and West, releasing all your teachers. The ceremony moves us on the wheel from the work of the West to the North.

Come back the next morning and begin the day with 7-7-7 breathing. This quiets the mind and body in preparation for a journey. When your mind is steady, then journey for a lost part of your soul that is now in grace to help with the work of the North.

As I traveled to the Lower World to find a lost part of myself to help me now, *I dove through the fissure of rock, through the Earth, to a stream where I was cleansed, floating down, down to a pool surrounded by rocks and hills, yet open to my garden. Went to the boulder. I met Huascar, today in the form of a winged horse. A future that is bright, multicolored, swirling, and gentle to open my third eye. A soft image of a baby clinging to me. To care for her is to love and open to this work. It was she who was to guide me on this path, and she was left behind at birth. Then was not her time, but now she will help me to allow the changes, the opening needed to walk into the me that Angus and Zoe know I should be. Coming back, Huascar was a white elephant, then a unicorn. Coming back into purple, reds, oranges, and light. Very beautiful, strong energy; very enveloping but not clinging; gentle, and there. Remember! Heard a stadium of happy people in light. Circular breathing. Up from the Mother and through the Tan Tien and out to the Mother. I again met Muki, that mischievous elemental spirit of the Earth who helps us to dig deeply. I came back.*

The lesson learned in this journey: Do not forget to "be" in nature. Connect. Listen. Smell. Feel. Hear. Be. Feel the energies. Perception in the North is allowing the be-coming. We can call off the search and remember our connection is with the ancient wisdom. Remember the circular breath. Begin to engage the unknowable. We can know and experience the unknowable, but only after it is experienced. Begin to remember. Take a quantum leap into the greater awareness. Be the essence of yourself. Take yourself out of the equation and allow yourself to be fully seen. Let there be congruence between who you say you are and who you are. Allow yourself to be who you are <u>now</u>. You are no longer your old stories. The stories are the stories. You are now your authentic self. As our shadows heal the stories, we become invisible.

Break free of the grip of time. Time keeps you bound to fate, and it is deadening the past. Keep in front of you the <u>now</u>. The day after the <u>now</u> is invisible. As you do this work, your destiny will be clearer to you. Energy = volume x mass^2 (MC^2). All the past (the mass) weighs you down and is sluggish. As you do this work, you release some of the mass, the sluggishness, and the heaviness. The destiny paths become revealed, the velocity of these paths accelerates, and things manifest almost instantly. When your field gets clear, all the light energy can flood in. Your old stuff is the fertilizer/mulch to grow the new. Watch your language and wording now. See what that lost soul piece has brought to you. Step out of time. Step toward the past and bring something back to change the present. Then you can step into the future and affect it.

Synchronicity becomes 99% of our awareness. Recognize when things are flowing. The world of cause and effect is ending.

You step into a sacred world because you are living in alignment and because you are sacred. You are no longer a physical being having a spiritual experience, but rather a spiritual being having a physical experience.

Exercise. Find a lovely sit spot to create your Nature Painting. If you were a four-legged, where would you go on this type of day? Walk for a while, really seeing. Open your belly. Every step you take is purposeful. Be aware of your body's alignment. Your skeleton supports your body. Where is your body when you walk? How do you feel? What is your alignment? Our bodies mirror that which we have been doing a long time. How are you walking on the Earth? Pay attention to your body in the air. Be aware.

Create a Nature Painting to work with your roles in life. The Nature Painting will allow the roles to be released into the mythic. Open Sacred Space, and create a border for your painting. Leave a little opening in the East to bring new energy in and to release old energies. Open your Wiracocha and write down all the roles you play, both positive and negative. Use the roles where you are <u>now</u>, not from the past. For me, that meant I could use: "I am a gentle spirit; a teacher; wicked and wonderful; an artist; a musician; a hard worker; a wife." I could abandon those created for me by others in the past: "I am mean, cruel, and rotten to the core; a victim; a martyr; stupid; fat; etc." These are roles you have in this life <u>now</u>. Roles in which you participate; roles you play; how you navigate the world at this time. Do the obvious first (*e.g.*, wife, daughter, caregiver, great aunt, mother to dogs, friend of horses, teacher, writer, gardener, reader), then more subtle (*e.g.*, healer/fixer, warrior, cook, etc.).

Roles

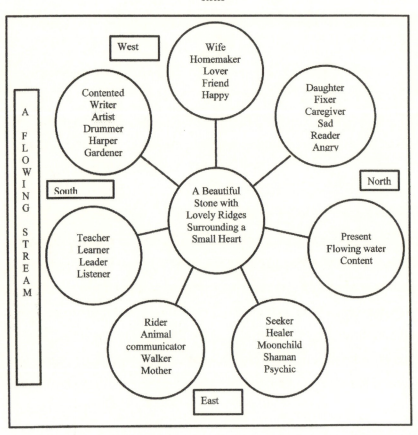

Wife
Homemaker
Lover
Friend
Happy

West

Contented
Writer
Artist
Drummer
Harper
Gardener

Daughter
Fixer
Caregiver
Sad
Reader
Angry

North

South

A Beautiful
Stone with
Lovely Ridges
Surrounding a
Small Heart

Present
Flowing water
Content

A
F
L
O
W
I
N
G
S
T
R
E
A
M

Teacher
Learner
Leader
Listener

Rider
Animal
communicator
Walker
Mother

Seeker
Healer
Moonchild
Shaman
Psychic

East

Think about your life, your roles, your wants and desires, your true self. Choose a stone that represents your true essence. Blow that true essence into the stone and place it in the middle of the painting. Give a gift of tobacco or corn to the sit spot and to the painting. Leave your painting for a while and let it rest.

The Nature Painting allows your physical body to remember its healed state. In your Luminous Body is a blueprint holding "you" in a state of perfection. If you have a continuing health, emotional, or spiritual problem, the "perfect" you is still in your field waiting to be discovered. But, as well as that state of perfection, your field may also hold a blueprint of things that happened in the past that are dense and stuck, allowing things like tumors, headaches, illness to come back. In this cosmology, this can be present life or past life stuff. Your current body/field needs to be cleared so it can remember the healed state of <u>now</u>. When those old, stale blueprints are removed, the chance of whatever it is that ails you to return is greatly lessened. When the blueprint is gone, you need to continue with the clearing so the density does not return and again effect the body. Sit for a while and remember: "I AM THE HEALED STATE." The body remembers that state and will help to take you there. Before you or a friend or family member goes for a medical test, like a mammogram, for example, have your field cleared so any negative imprints are gone. When the imprint is gone, the body can heal and the cycle of more medical tests and procedures may be prevented. Clear the field before whatever "it" is, becomes locked into it. When the field is clear, the physical body often remains clear, as well. This does not mean you should substitute energy clearing for medical tests and procedures, however.

Now, return to your painting. On the way, collect burnable materials that you can place in the painting to represent your roles. Consider how these roles relate to one another, and place them in the appropriate grouping into the painting. Choose a second North stone to represent your roles. Map the roles on paper. Rearrange them on paper until you are content they are in the proper place in the painting. Then, take something to represent each role and hold it in your left hand. Hold the stone in your right hand. Think about that role. Bring up that energy in you that is that role. Focus, and then follow it or track it into the past, and then into the future. See the role dissolving into the future. Blow that role into the stone. Place the item you are holding into the painting to represent that role. Repeat this process with all of your roles. This will take some time. Place your second stone in the painting surrounded by all your roles.

If you are working with a partner, share your map of the painting. Be the witness to your partner. Do not interpret. What are the hidden roles/the blind spot that you do not see about yourself? If something comes back later, go and add it to the painting. A representation of my sand painting appears on page 102.

I was sitting next to a lovely stream, facing the West. I sat with my painting and reviewed the roles and their relationships. I opened my medicine pouch and held each item there, as well. Bear: Watch for me now in your dreams Little Sister. I will carry you far. Beaver: Home, health, care is fine. Love above all. Forgiveness. Forgiveness in light. Larimer: The water, clear, and flowing. Kyanite: The blue door through which my true power lies is opening. Be present; pay attention. Pearl: Soft love; honor your relationships. Chrysocolla: Dark lungs cleared and off the energy body replaced by strength and muscle and light. Fluorite: Into the water, clarity and brightness. Now is fine!

Draw a tarot card as a way to see where you are <u>now</u>. Look at the picture and really see. Do not look up the meaning of the card. Just let the picture inform you. As an example, the card I pulled was "the Hermit." It seemed to tell me: *Support from spirit; a lot of fish to be caught; a lot to gather; a lot to be gained. Time to really concentrate on the fullness of what you have. Sit with this for a while. Father of Earth. Father of Water. Father of Air. A hermit, going within, cooking. A full moon and grizzly bear in the background.*

The purpose of this work is to illuminate your roles and separate you from them at the same time. We are not our roles. Sometimes, the roles are "shoulds" or "have-tos," and by recognizing those, they may become more acceptable. It is different when it is your nature to be helpful and "do for others," but when you "have to," it may not belong to you. For example, let's say your grandfather abused you when you were a child. Now, he is old and in a nursing home. Your parents say: "You have to visit your grandfather. You may not have another chance." Should you go? Do you have to? Will going make you more whole and provide something you need in your life? Or, have you already made peace and going just placates your parents? Is making your parents happy something you "have to" or "should" do? Be aware of what's going on when you are faced with these kinds of choices.

Placing your roles, and all that is part of those roles, into the stone, works at the mythic level. When the items representing those roles go to the fire, they are transformed at the energetic level. This is very focused and intense work, and it will help you to find your true nature.

We now begin our work again in the three centers of connectivity: Yachay, Munay, and Llankay. Three diamonds whose points connect as one shifts to the next center may represent these. The chakras also move within these centers. In the bottom triangle of the Lower World are the root and sacral chakras. The solar plexus joins this center to the Middle World, with the heart chakra in the center. Connecting the Middle World to the Upper World is the throat chakra. The third eye is in the center of the Upper World, and, at the very top, the crown chakra. The chakras are in these centers, holding the Luminous Body around the physical body.

In the Peruvian cosmology, as well as the three centers of connectivity, there are three centers of exchange:

1. Literal, in the belly (the flow, Serpent, Amaru);

2. Symbolic, in the heart (connectivity, rainbow light Jaguar, Chocochinchi); and,

3. Mythic, the third eye (framework/vision, Eagle/Condor, Apuchin).

In the perceptual state of Eagle/Condor, Apuchin, the visionary, at the third eye, one learns to detach and rise/fly high above with awareness. There, the "big picture" is revealed. Flying above the Earth provides an overview, and, from that perspective, one can see how we (and others) walk in the world. From this place, we see, without emotion, but with great clarity, the structure and framework of how we are living in the world around us. At the level of Chocochinchi, Jaguar, nothing is as it seems. All is at the level of emotion and connectivity to all paths. Everything is always changing. It is difficult to recognize what is "true" or "real" at this level of awareness. At the level of Serpent, Amaru, again, there is no emotion. Everything is as it is. In this view, one sees only the literal flow. But at the top of the diamonds, above the level of Apuchin, is the eighth chakra—the transpersonal point, that holds all the chakras in place, all can be given up to Spirit. POOF. Poof to the Void. Give whatever the issue is to Spirit.

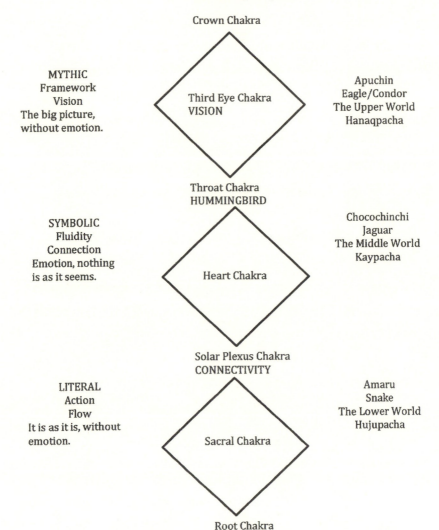

POOF
Give the issue up to Spirit

Crown Chakra

MYTHIC
Framework
Vision
The big picture,
without emotion.

Third Eye Chakra
VISION

Apuchin
Eagle/Condor
The Upper World
Hanaqpacha

Throat Chakra
HUMMINGBIRD

SYMBOLIC
Fluidity
Connection
Emotion, nothing
is as it seems.

Heart Chakra

Chocochinchi
Jaguar
The Middle World
Kaypacha

Solar Plexus Chakra
CONNECTIVITY

LITERAL
Action
Flow
It is as it is, without
emotion.

Sacral Chakra

Amaru
Snake
The Lower World
Hujupacha

Root Chakra
FLOW

Exercise: To see where information comes into your field. Open your Wiracocha. Clear at the crown. Move your awareness to the level of Serpent.

I saw: *Angus, my dog, old, sleepy on the floor. Itchy, hurting/ sleeping, me care giving, tired, sad.*

Clear at the crown. Take a deep breath. Shift your awareness to Jaguar.

I saw my boy again: *Angus, ready but holding on. Deep sadness, loss, fear, grief, more grief, then pain, loss. YIKES!*

Clear at the crown chakra. Move to Eagle/Condor.

At the level of the visionary: *Angus flying across the meadow. Me, running at his side. Joy and movement. Zoe too when she is ready. No pain. Just being.*

Clear at the crown. POOF, give it all to spirit.

Notice how the stories live in Jaguar. Being in Jaguar will not/does not help. Being in the state of emotion does not help. The Eagle/Condor state will help. The Serpent state can also be <u>practical</u>. At Jaguar is the high-speed come apart. At Eagle/Condor is peace and joy. These levels are the way we engage with the world. Often, we are reacting without awareness of what we are doing, seeing, becoming. Therefore, shift. Be present. Be aware of the level at which you are engaging. Too literal? Shift to Jaguar.

Too emotional there? Shift to Eagle/Condor. Then shift again and "POOF," giving all the emotion and confusion up to Spirit.

Exercise. Deconstruction. Deconstruct a "loaded" word or some issue you would like to resolve that you can describe/ define with one word. Is a major event, like a marriage or divorce, happening in your life? Would you like more information about a new job, a relationship? Find a word that describes what is happening. Then go into each of the levels of awareness and actually "become" that word. Pay attention to your body and your breath as you move through each of the levels. You may want to ask a friend to support you so you do not crash into a wall or piece of furniture.

Open your Wiracocha. Note that whenever you open your Wiracocha, you are in double Sacred Space. In each state of awareness, keep repeating your word out loud. Say it over and over. Bring up the feeling of whatever you are working with really is. Watch from Serpent—do not judge or interpret. Watch from Jaguar—do not engage. Watch from Eagle/Condor—the big picture. Poof, and release the experience to Spirit.

This process is rather like diagramming a sentence in a literature class. Instead of a sentence, your experience diagrams each word through each of the three levels/states of awareness.

As an example, I chose to work with the feeling of being blocked. *Blocked. In Serpent, I felt heavy; pushed down; blocked. Others observed I was slow with just head movement. Looking around. My body moved very little, head almost to the ground.*

Jumped up into Jaguar. Scratching at a fast pace, circular motion.
I felt caged. Jumped to Eagle/Condor. Up on my toes. From Eagle/
Condor, I perched and looked at a river flowing freely. I didn't stay
in Eagle/Condor long enough. I want to stay forever and not come
back.

Exercise. Finding the Healed Face. The Shaman's way of
seeing is a pointed focus to see the literal first, then the shift to
Jaguar, and then a shift that lands in Eagle/Condor. In this exercise,
you shift your way of seeing your partner's face, and as you do,
you may look at the person (or yourself) with a new perspective.
With a partner (or with a mirror looking at yourself), look left eye
to left eye. The Shaman, perhaps a third person (or a recording),
rattles and guides: "Serpent state, see the literal face. Breathe out
serpent. Go to Jaguar. See with the eye of Jaguar. Release. Go to
Eagle/Condor. Watch as the face shifts. All of a sudden, one face
stays: the healed face. What you see in the other person's eye, or
in the mirrored eye of yourself, are projected faces of you. Using
the other person's eye helps you to see yourself. Remember the
qualities of the last face—this is your fulfilled self.

As I gazed into my partner's left eye, I saw a face I knew
well and then I shifted. *In Serpent, I saw a smooth boulder with a*
"toe-hold" place for the eye. In Jaguar, I saw a boulder, an animal
with yellow fur, and a grooved and aged rock with a knowing eye.
In Eagle/Condor, I saw a smile of contentment in an older female
with deep eyes and a gentle solidness. These all felt right to me.

Exercise. In this exercise, you can use either a real person or
an imaginary spirit guide as your partner. With your partner, track

111

through the three centers of exchange. One-person acts as "tracker." The other person acts as "client." The client raises a question on which he/she needs guidance. The tracker opens his/her Wiracocha three times over her/himself and over his/her partner and then expands into Luminous Awareness, at the same time remaining grounded. The tracker is bringing attention through Luminous Awareness to each center in the client to find the answers to the question. It is for the client to interpret what those answers mean.

The tracker brings his/her right hand toward his or her own belly, creating awareness at the level of the Serpent. The tracker then extends the hand toward the client. The tracker will receive information as a word, feeling, smell, picture, shape or color, in Serpent. Then the tracker moves the hand to his/her heart to create awareness in Chocochinchi, and then extends his/her hand toward the client. When an "answer" is received, the hand moves to the tracker's third eye. When awareness shifts, the hand is again extended toward the client. Being detached from the information, report it to the client who can create meaning from the answers.

As an example, I did not have a partner for this exercise but I had a question I very much wanted to be answered. *I decided to track with angelic beings and myself. I asked the question: "Where do I source a song for North America—a new song, not Native American, but something else to welcome the Apus here in the North?" First, in my belly, I saw a huge mouth with many huge, white teeth smiling. In my heart center, I saw myself upstairs in a dark room. In my third eye, I saw my Peacock helpers in beautiful shimmering green light. When the exercise was repeated, I got the words: rock, sun, and ocean. I saw images of a doorway in the clouds, a stairway from the bottom of the ocean to the top of the water. It was like focusing on the top of the sky.*

Pachamama hear me calling
Shimmer here atop the sky
Shimmer here beneath the ocean
Be here now and warm your hands.

Ausangate hear me calling
The deep green doorway opens here
Over rocks, through clouds and sunshine
Strength we need here at the fire.

Huaca Wilka hear me calling.
Your large smile lights the sky.
Down the stairway in the sunshine,
Warm your body by our fire.

Mama Killia hear me calling.
Softly light our path tonight.
Be here. Hold me gently
At the fire here tonight.

Apus, Apus, hear me calling.
Surround my space with your strong hands.
Prayer here, and love, will feed you.
Waken now from your deep slumber.
Welcome, Welcome Beings of Light.

Journeying to the Upper World

When traveling to the Upper World, there are four levels (Bardo planes) where souls may continue their spiritual journey and work. First is the level of the stone people. It is dark there and takes a longer time to process one's issues. Stones have a very long life span. Next is the plant kingdom, the place of plant spirit medicine. There you can talk to plant spirits and ask how they may help you or others in healing. Third is the animal kingdom, a place in which further healing may be done. Do not engage with animals you may have known or people you may encounter in the land of the stone people, plants, or animals. They are there to process and learn, and it is not for us to interfere.

Fourth is the level of whales, dolphins, and other beings with individual souls. In this cosmology, people, whales, dolphins, dogs, and frogs have individual souls. Other animals and plants, although they may have individual personalities and appear as individuals (like cats or horses or elephants) in form, are always part of a collective soul. At this level, you may engage with loved ones or friends who have recently passed. Indeed, when they realize you are taking this journey, they may come to meet you here. From the level of dolphins and whales, you may go up a ladder to a fifth, highly spiritual plane. Here, you can meet your "original" parents or commune with spirit guides or angels.

Exercise. Journey to the Upper World to explore. The first time, do not take this journey on your own. Ask someone who is experienced with journeying to guide you. Open your Wiracocha. You are going to journey to the Upper World with the intention of exploring. Go to the cave of Jaguar. Call on Jaguar. Humpui Otoronga (Hum-pwee O-toe-rong-a). Come, Mother/Sister Jaguar. Go into the back of the cave. Ask Jaguar to dismember you. Your physical body will stay in the cave, and your Luminous Body, surrounded by light, goes up. Notice your spirit body go up in a lovely cylinder of light. You are light, traveling in an elevator of light. At the level of the Stone People, ask one of your stones to be with you. Do not engage there.

When I first visited: *There was a shaft of light—my arms rose, and I took my red stone and walked into the stone kingdom. It was warm, dark, and flowing. I felt like I had come home.*

Go back to the elevator of light and go up to the Plant Kingdom. In the plant kingdom, take a plant spirit guardian with you. Do not engage there.

While there, *I saw blades of grass, flowers, and tall, strong trees. Phantoms though. People also seemed to be there.*

Go back to the elevator of light to the animal kingdom. Take a power animal with you. Here you may acknowledge others but do not engage with people or any of your own animals, like a past pet, you might find there. You can talk to other animals if you have questions, but not your own! *My Giraffe friend came with me. There were herds and herds of animals.*

Go back to the elevator of light to the fourth level. At the fourth level, you may engage with your ancestors, friends, and others who have passed. Those who have healed and not yet reincarnated may be there. *I did not see any people, but I swam with the dolphins, and it was grand.*

From here notice a golden ladder. This ladder leads to the fifth dimension. Climb up and ask the gatekeeper, Pacha Kuti, if you may pass. Tell him it is your intent to explore. Ask your light parents or guardian angel to accompany you.

There is much to learn at each level. Journey to the Lower World when you need help with Earthly problems, or wish to work with your power animal. Sometimes, you will work with Huascar, but you might also work with Muki, especially for soul retrieval. When you need help with spiritual issues, journey to the Upper World.

Exercise. Journey to the fifth level of guides and masters. There, Pacha Kuti is the gatekeeper. Again, go to the cave of Jaguar and ask to be dismembered. Enter the cylinder of light and go past the Bardo planes. Be aware of the different worlds as you travel up the elevator.

At the level of the Stone People, it is browner and warmer. At the level of the Plant People, a huge tree helps me go up and up, through the animal kingdom to the ancestral level. Again, I saw no ancestors but many dolphins. I received a *message from Orca. "Remember the Star People. Spend time outside at night." Purple night; galaxies opening.*

At the fourth level, look across the landscape and see a ladder. It is only four or five steps. Climb up and ask Pacha Kuti, the gatekeeper, to guide you. Ask to meet your original, spiritual parents. Ask your spiritual parents for a message about your essential self.

Here, *I walked up the ladder to the fifth level. It was so high, and there was much singing. My parents were square and solid—Stone People! They said: Orion Remember Cassiopeia, All the Star People (ORCA). They handed me a light-filled stone. It filled my heart. I was called back.*

Exercise. Go to your Nature Painting. Open your Wiracocha three times over yourself and three times over your painting. Take the stone in the center and blow into it your essential self. Hold your stone. Rattle and meditate on your essential self.

As I rattled, much about my life became clear to me. *The ladder I have been seeing all my life leads to the Upper World. I came from the stones. I have lived as a great whale and communed with dolphins. Bees and ants came to help me with my painting. Water flows nearby. The stone from the Gobi desert lies to the left of my essential self. It is done. I added to my painting this morning a small brilliant red leaf and nine other fall leaves. It is done. The gift of the Shaman is to engage in dialog with all life.*

Cut loose from old and limiting beliefs. Now you can journey to the Upper World with protection and access plant spirit medicine. The plant spirit ally is what can help heal, not necessarily the literal plant itself. However, do not engage with other humans or other creatures/beings that do not belong in the plant kingdom. Do commune with the medicine.

Take your second stone and blow into it all this new information about yourself. Then, using that stone and a nearby small stick, you will unravel all your roles into the future. You will unravel all your roles until they no longer exist. Take a stone and blow the essence of yourself into the stone. Then, pick up the items representing your roles. Hold these in your hand, and, while in Luminous Awareness, rattle and journey. See the role unravel. This is a Middle World journey. Let each role unravel until you see its end. Go beyond death until it dissipates in the ether. The roles hold us, but we want them NOT to bind us. Do this at all three levels of engagement: Serpent, Jaguar, and Eagle/Condor. Allow the roles to unravel until they are gone. By unraveling your roles until they end, you take the "charge" and the "have to" out of the roles. You have a choice now to do or not to do. Once you release the role, sometimes the new doing of that role becomes fun, even pleasant! For example, one of your roles may be that of "wife." Some of the tasks you perform in that role are "should dos," and some are "have tos." Once you see how that role unravels, and once you know which are your "should do," and which your "have tos," you can regain joy in the role. Your essence and true nature then remains, and the "role" works for you again. You recover your true nature. When done with that role, stamp your foot three times and place the stone and roles outside of the painting.

While I was processing my roles, *I journeyed back to my essential self, processing and adding all that I learned this morning. As each role extended to the past and into the future, a different aspect was revealed. Each unraveling moved at a different speed with a different pattern or color.*

Take what you want to cleanse. Go to the fire. Do a clearing. Release the roles into the fire and burn them as needed. Release them with gratitude into the fire while stating, "I release this role to the end." The strand to which the role was attached is a Ceke strand you follow to the end. When done, stamp your foot again three times. It is done. The way you walk in that role is done, too.

Through your Lineage Stone, the work of the South connected your Mesa to all Mesas. The work in the West, with your intent, connected your stones to the Pampamesayoq, to the energetic lineage of the Earthkeepers. The next ceremony creates, in the work of the North, a connection of your Mesa to the Altomesayoq, the high rites connecting to the Apus. You are connected with supernatural beings. With ceremony and by letting go of your roles, you can step out of time. In knowing some of the secrets you have kept from yourself (and you now know a whole lot of secrets), you are moving toward the healed state.

Exercise and Journey. Take your third stone. This is your Destiny Stone. Blow your essence into that stone and rattle to the fifth level. Envision your life as if you were moving down a tunnel. There are many threads or strands of energy in this "momentum tunnel." In the tunnel, you can follow one strand for a while and then move to another. Over time, this tunnel of our life gets over-stuffed. In this work, we begin to clear some of those strands out, removing the density and clutter from the tunnel. This clearing creates more space to move. As the number of strands lessens, space is created between them. A few of those strands become destiny strands. Destiny strands are not held so tightly. With them you can see who you are becoming, and things can happen much more quickly.

Journey. Look at your life's purpose as if it were a box, or tube, or a tunnel. Through that tunnel, many possibilities are flowing. Each possibility represents a filament of potential destiny. Some strands flow from the past. Some flow into the future. Some strands are shorter. Some are very thick. Some are thinner. The "Destiny Tunnel" contains all of life's infinite variety and all of the possibilities. However, your soul's purpose has only one or two that exist to show you how to walk in the world, in the <u>now</u>, in the form you now occupy. Your task, in this journey, is to identify a strand that opens many possibilities in your life.

Destiny Tunnel in a Cluttered Luminous Field

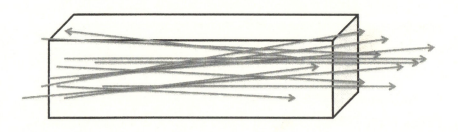

Destiny Tunnel in a Clear Luminous Field

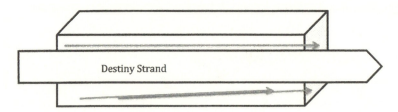

Ask for a destiny strand to be shown to you. Say: "Show me the possibilities," or, "Show me the path that serves my highest good," or, "Show me the destiny where I live totally in the healed state." Think about this as thoughts manifest so fast after this work. You barely have time to think about something, and it happens. Outside of the momentum tunnel now are strands that go up with infinite possibilities because old stuff is no longer pushing us in other directions. Now, there is space in your field so you can access your destiny. Your destiny now shows the quality of *you* and how you walk in the world. It is your soul's purpose on Earth in this life. Over time, you can continue to journey with your Destiny Stone. Now, record your journey. Place the stone in the painting.

Later, at the fire, make a vow about something you want to do with your purpose in being here or your life's purpose. My vow was *"to walk my destiny with patience and joy so as to live my physical life as fully and completely as possible while showing others their way. I am among animals. I walk softly on the Earth."*

At bedtime, set the intention to dream about what you need to remember about your Destiny. My dreamtime is usually disjointed, and I do not remember much. For this dreamtime: *I could not sleep at first. I got up five times during the night. After midnight I was aware of a deep and peaceful sleep. I was at the fire. Behind my house, a dirt road led deep into a wood up a hill. Many people were dancing and singing. Gifts were given. My gift was a pair of crystal shoes. They each weighed 11 or 12 pounds, but when I put them on they merged into my feet, and I could glide across the Earth. They did not weigh me down. That is what I was to remember.*

121

We are bringing ourselves into proper alignment. We no longer stand in cause and effect, but as we are. Singing to the Apus strengthens one's connections to them. A collective Mesa is created after and through your personal healing Mesa. Remember the Santa Tierras, the Earth spirits, the Fairy realm. Ask your guides, the Earth, the mountains or your fifth-world spirits for help and guidance. Those completely out of the Apus can manifest in the third dimension as well as the fifth.

Exercise. A fire ceremony to honor your roles and transform them. At the fire ceremony you create this evening, you step into and accept the place that has been held for you for a very long time. This is the night you are ready to meet the night and the fire on your own terms. You have released yourself, your ancestors, and your roles. You have now raised your vibration to the level of the fire. Tonight, you will kneel and present yourself directly to Spirit. Think about what kind of a ceremony or gift you would like to make to the fire in terms of your path, and the collective of which you are now a part. It is time to look deep within and see what truly speaks to you. You have learned much on this journey, and things are now much clearer. The lineage comes to you through your Mesa, through all those who have completed this path before you, through those who have been to the mountains and experienced rites there. Your stones now connect through the Cekes to their place of origin and with other stones who have been awakened.

Tonight, create a ceremony to transform your North stones. First, fill an aluminum turkey-roasting pan with sand. Go to your Nature Painting, and gather your stones and other items from the painting you wish to burn. Scatter the remaining parts of the painting. Place your first two stones into the sand. Light your fire. Sing and chant. See the fire become friendly. Take a flower to represent all your roles. Give gratitude and release all that remains into the flower. Release the flower to the fire with other burnables from your painting. All that now burns transforms you, as well. Kneel before the fire. Take your place there as a medicine man or woman. Your focus is soft. You are now a wisdom keeper. Remember this. Drop your third stone into the center of the fire as you say: "As I take my place as a wisdom keeper, I *vow* to take care of the Earth." Or, create your own sacred vow.

The stones go through the fire on your behalf, and sometimes they go out of time. Their transformation transforms your energy centers, and that transformed energy now enters your Mesa. Stay with your fire until it is pretty much out. The next morning, come back and see how your stones have transformed. In a state of ceremony, welcome your stones to your Mesa by tapping each stone against the others. Create a feeling of welcome and joy as you add them to your altar.

The mountain rights earned in working with the North are the Wisdom Keeper's rights. Now, through the various perceptual states, you can see the Cekes begin to form. You can see the Cekes source from all that is the collective: the Earth, the stars, and the sun. You become a link in the chain of knowledge. You are anchored to the mountains. Your energy becomes more refined. As you step into the path of lightening and fire, the path of transformation, the bell ringing is the lightening. Your Lineage Stone (a gift from your teacher or a special stone created by you in ceremony) connects you to the bloodline of the Andes, the collective intelligence. It will source you to the collective through that mountain of its birth. You are now a spiritual being having a physical experience. Step into joy; step into unconditional joy. Understand that joy comes from within you. Although joy can surround you with feelings of wonder and happiness, happiness by itself means something had to happen. Now separateness and duality stop, and you are one in the <u>now</u>.

Over the next few months, practice these steps to deepen your experience on the Shamanic path before you move to the final work in the East:

1. Create a Despacho for your Itu Apu, the mountain of your birth. If no mountain, then a nearby river or a lake. Go there, and let go of the place you were born. The spirit guarding the place you were born has supported you. Honor its support using materials created where you are now to come to closure with those powers that honored you in the beginning. Give gratitude for that spirit's help, and release yourself from its care.

2. Create a Despacho for your Ayllu Apu, for the mountain (lake or river) where you live. Anchor yourself where you are. Your support and protection come from here. Recognize those Ceke lines that support you, your village, who you are becoming.

3. Create four fire ceremonies to strengthen your connection with the Lineage Stone and your ancestors. Call on the Apus.

4. Journey.

5. Remember the Four Practices of the North work:

- Simplicity. Do not be possessed by your stuff. Do not let your "stuff" possess you. You now become effective in your roles because they no longer possess you. You are regaining of the innocence of birth, the simplicity of beginning afresh.

- Live consequentially. Every word, thought, and action creates and sends a vibration. Be aware of the consequences of what you say, think, and do.

- Invisibility. Be transparent. Walk your talk. Do not be a target for others to criticize or abuse. Choose being useful and valuable.

- Not knowing. Engage your life as a love. Be in a state of gratitude. Bring freshness to each moment. Do not be encumbered by what you think are the facts. Go to the wisdom. Shift perceptual states. Keep up your work on ceremony. Create your own ceremony. Go into the mythic and do what you need to do at the energetic level.

Remember: "Worry is what we do to manifest what we do not want!" The Universe will go out of its way to take care of you. As is said at http://tut.com: "Thoughts become things. Think good ones!"

As we move to the work of the East, integrating the knowledge, we will learn how we walk in the world as a seer. We will dream the worlds into being and receive the Star Rites.

You are now ready to begin to work with your Shaman's Lineage Stone. Whether your stone was a gift or one created by the transformative power of the Nature Painting, this stone is now your connection to the collective. Sit with it. Light a candle outside. Open your Mesa in Sacred Space. Place your Kuyas around you. Open your Wiracocha three times. The stone will show the sacred line to an aspect of creation. Open your belly counterclockwise. Start at the outer layer of your field. Breathe, pumping breath into your belly. Pull/source from Amaru, from the flow. Receive the knowing at that level—pull in, in, until your hands rest on the belly. Again, at the heart level, pull through the layers and see with the knowing of Jaguar. Again at the third eye, see like the Eagle/Condor and bring the stone through all the layers of your Luminous Body. Journal it. Introduce your stone to your Mesa by gently tapping it upon the other stones. Do a fire ceremony to honor it! Use all the burnables from the Nature Painting and smudge your new stone in the smoke of the fire as you waft your Mesa through the smoke.

Exercise. To send others safely on a journey.

As well as a tool of personal growth and insight, your Mesa can be used to bless others. The following little prayer is designed to keep people safe while traveling. You must have a full Mesa of 12 stones (or four people with three stones or two people with six stones). Form a circle around the person being blessed. Hold your

Mesa in both hands. Starting at the person's feet and moving up the body with each push (ending at the crown), push your Mesa toward the person nine times as you chant: Kuti (coo-tee), Kuti, Kuti. Ana Karina (ann-ah ka-reen-ah), Ana Karina, Ana Karina; Yoksey (yoke-see), Yoksey, Yoksey. On the final "Yoksey," turn to the outer edge of the circle, away from the person, and blow toward your Mesa as it reaches toward the sky. Repeat three times. The person will arrive safely. Travelers are now safe on the journey home.

The "homework" for the North requires much more preparation and thought than asked for in the other directions. If you now live far from the place of your birth, you will need to plan a trip back. If that place is not one where you are able to light a fire (as mine was in the center of a city on one of the Great Lakes), what are your options? If you do not live, and never have lived, close to mountains, from where do you source? I figured out that Lake Michigan supported me at birth, and that the Mississippi River has taken over. Journey for help and ask for instructions in creating these Despachos. The Despacho I created for my Itu Apu, the Apu of my birth, Lake Michigan was very different. I began by blessing and clearing rainwater. I was creating a Despacho of sacred water. I opened Sacred Space, and added to the water:

1. a piece of Fluorite from Hardin County where I spent my teen years,

2. a Stone found recently who asked to go,

3. a broken piece of my Destiny Stone,

4. three shells given to me by my Ayllu,

5. ash from Peruvian incense, and

6. a small feather given to me by a friend who raises chickens. I first used the feather to bless space around my home with prayers and singing.

All this was placed in a jar. When I arrived at the Lake, it was easy to open Sacred Space, say my prayers, and pour the whole in the Lake. A different ceremony was created for the River, who now supports me, but it was another ceremony based on water.

My dreamtime after the ceremonies were completed was so real and pertinent to the work. *It was night. A hungry Jaguar walked the streets of my dream, and I locked my door against her and saw people on a hillside being murdered and the red blood spilling. Then I could see myself sleeping. I went back to the house and called to the Jaguar and opened the door. I took her into my heart and fed her a dozen scrambled eggs and a gallon of milk. She was content and gave me a vision of such beauty this morning that I am in awe still. I was riding in the car. We passed a series of low trees with large nests. At first, I thought they were hawks but no—peacocks. As I watched, a beautiful hen came up, her feathers softly brown, her wings heavy with rain or dew. Beside her rose her male child—iridescent, shimmering hues of blue, and they held each other, wings out-spread and swayed and danced in the sun. Several others in nests were also showing lovely feathers, but these two who were dancing were amazingly lovely. See our dance; join and sway; colors fill the sky; our song wakes the day!*

I journeyed and was asked to write a brief "creation story." *There was light, white/yellow/pink, full of love and joy and intelligence. The light danced and sang and knew great joy, but also loneliness. The light formed a word, and with the word was creation. The light created companions for itself, and more words were formed and shaped the form the words created. And the world coalesced around this light and incorporated itself into all the elements. The light is joy and love, and is everywhere if one but looks.*

FIVE

The East: Transit to the Source

You will need: three stones whose birthplace you know.

Now it is time to move to the East, Eagle/Condor/Apuchin. It is the time of transit to the Source. On the Shaman's Path, as our vibration increases, our resolve to move to the next state moves us in the direction in which we need to go. In the South, we shed that which no longer serves us, "as the serpent sheds her skin." We answered the questions: "Where is the block? What do we need to let go?" The work of the South was in the lower three chakras (root, sacral, and the solar plexus) and connected us to Jaguar. After that work was completed and processed, our new state of being again becomes restrictive. It is time to step on the wheel and move again to shed that skin. Now, we have the tools to do this. Working with our Mesas, our stones, Nature Paintings, creating ceremonies, and looking at the world through a Shaman's eyes, we know how to step out of the wheel to transform. In the West, we identify those final themes that need to be shed and remove those that block the flow. The work of the West allows you to remove themes not yet shed, removing any that block the flow.

In the West, Jaguar medicine, we looked at our own shadows, our connection to others, the ancestors. We worked with the heart chakra. In the North, Hummingbird gave voice to our throat chakra. Here we worked with our third eye and learned to see. In tonight's fire, what do you want to release to be fully present?

What do you need to know as you move to the work of the East and learn to become the Visionary? Ask for awareness in the dreamtime.

My dreamtime for a change was full of joy. *The dream messages were all about joy. The first two passed quickly and left me with joy. The third time I entered the dream state, I was in my maternal grandparents' old house. No one seemed to be there, and I went into their bedroom and opened a drawer. It was full of hankies with my Grandpa's name embroidered there—Henry. I left and was walking down the sidewalk by their house and found a long tattered feather—then more—more—a handful of feathers, more than enough for everyone here. Vulture—rebirth—rebirth and renewed health is at hand. A time of endings and beginnings. Trust the process for your benefit.*

Exercise. A Meditation. Center. Open to infinity in the South. Center. Open to infinity in the West. Center. Open to infinity in the North. Center. Open to infinity in the East. Center. Open to infinity in the Earth below. Center. Open to infinity in the Sky above. Center. Open to infinity in all directions. Be aware that all is one.

Journey. Intention: Journey through the Tree of Life to the Upper World.

In this journey, Peacock carried me *through the membrane into a brilliant light. A horse and rider came into view—freedom to choose and to be is the message. Remembrance of air/wind/ motion, and physical control, and spiritual flight. That part of me that was lost came into my heart. If I do this work, what I desire will come to pass. My purpose fulfilled. I tend to be lazy and must consciously choose to work instead. Day by day, each day, I must choose to work.*

Exercise. Find a new sit spot. Open Sacred Space. Open your Wiracocha. Create a new Nature Painting. Create a large painting and within it, five smaller circles. Leave the door to the East open. All of your stones will be placed in the painting. Place your East stones in the eastern-most small circle with your Lineage Stone, the Inka stone or the Shaman's stone you created in ceremony when you began this path. Place your North stones in the northern-most small circle. Place your West stones in the western-most small circle. Place your South stones in the southern-most small circle. Place something in the center of the painting to represent yourself. Leave the stones to rest.

Come back to your painting a few hours later. Remove your South stones one at a time. Ask each one if there is more dense energy that needs to transform. Recognize it. Going to each of the perceptual states, pull each stone to your belly. Hold it. Transform at each state. Be aware of what is shifting as the stores flow from your Luminous Body into the stone. Place it back in the painting so Spirit can work with it. In the South are the themes/stories of your life that you repeat. Shed them.

Go to the West. Remove your West stones one at a time and remember your ancestors. View each one through each of the perceptual states. These may be ancestral, DNA, or karmic themes. Differentiate them. Recognize them. Hold each stone at your heart center and process these parts of your past and future lives. Let Jaguar chew up remaining issues.

In the North, are there any roles you need to release? Take each stone, and review your roles. Are there new, related roles that need to be tracked? Follow them. Integrate them. Remember your destiny.

Leave your stones in the painting for a time of transformation and transcendence.

In the East, your new stones will now take on purpose as they become a Kuya in your Mesa. First, choose a stone from the East to be your Amaru Stone. That stone will transform and hold the energy of the flow. It will see where any remaining blocks can be removed. Second, choose a stone to hold the energy of Jaguar. Your Jaguar Stone holds the energy of Chocochinchi, that energy of connectivity. It will show you what you do is related to the world in which you want to live. Third, select a stone to represent Eagle/Condor. This stone, your vision, represents how you walk in the world. Your Lineage Stone, the stone that helped all the others to transform, now takes on another purpose. It connects you, and your Mesa, to the Source.

If you desire, you can add something to the painting. Whatever issue, theme, or story this item represents, blow it into the item. Blow into it to represent what you need to release. Later, take these items to the fire. In the work of the East, you are allowed to look at any projections keeping you from your true path.

Exercise. Open your Wiracocha. Track each stone from the Ceke line it is from back into your field with 7-7-7 breathing. This process will take you into Luminous Awareness. Ask that you be connected to Source through the stone. The stone brings new energy from Source into your Luminous Field. You are moving out to the "collective all" in the East. Pull that new energy into your belly, heart and third eye. Give it time to enter. This may take several breaths. Each may be different.

When you arrive at the stones of the East, bring your Amaru stones into your belly with 7-7-7 breathing. Place your Amaru Stone with those in the South. This stone, taken to Source, will re-inform those three. Bring your Chocochinchi Stone into your belly. Place your Chocochinchi Stone in the West. Bring your Apuchin Stone into your third eye. Place your Apuchin Stone in the North. Finally, hold your Shaman's Stone, now your Lineage Stone. Track it. Track it to its birthplace. Bring it into your belly, your heart, and your third eye. Let it inform your Mesa. Place this stone in the East, leaving the door open.

Amaru, the flow in the belly, contains the first three chakras where you work to remove blockages. Chocochinchi, the rainbow light warrior, Jaguar, takes us from this Pacha/time to the rainbow bridge to the next Pacha. Chocochinchi is connectivity and can be represented by the heart chakra. Apuchin, Condor/Eagle, show you the big picture. The throat, third eye, and crown chakras soar with Eagle/Condor. Use each stone. Track, holding your stones, from time to time. Remember that as new stories take over your daily life, you can take them to the stones and transform them. The work does not stop just because you have completed one full circle. The new stones of the East will take you from Source, beyond where you were before. Your Lineage Stone takes you out of time. It allows you to move backward and forward, and be in a state where it seems that time, as we generally think of it, does not exist. There is just you, being.

Exercise. A Three-Card Story. This exercise was completed at the beginning of our path. Now, it moves a few steps further. Tarot cards operate at the mythic level. The Nature Painting also moves the issues out to the energetic. Shifts take place fastest at the mythic and energetic. If you want to transform any issue in your life, it moves fastest at these two levels. Use Tarot cards to help tell your story.

Draw three cards and write a store in seven parts. The parts of the story are also a representation of how your chakras may be viewing this issue in your life. Part 1 is a sense of journey, the big picture, the root of the problem. Part 2 is the emotional element of the story. Where is the current energy? Is the energy waiting, stuck, integrating? Part 3, your intellect in the solar plexus, is about obstructions, lacks, or gifts. What does your gut tell you about this part of the story? Part 4 is for Shadow, aspects of you in each character (pluses or minuses you do not recognize about yourself). This is Chocochinchi energy, the part that connects the whole. Part 5 shows the back doors. What holds you back, and prevents you from stepping into your power? Part 6 allows you to look at limiting beliefs. Is there a "should" do or a "have" to do here? Are you working with someone else's projection for you? What does your third eye really want to say? Part 7, the end of the story, is the binding piece. This piece creates a new map. Now that you have taken your story to the mythic and energetic levels, how are you walking in the world? When working with the cards, view yourself as a part of the cards, as you would see yourself as a part of a dream.

My Story. The Reluctant Shaman. Once upon a time, there was a reluctant Shaman. She had been at the center of the world, and everything she wanted flowed into her. Snake surrounded her, and her energy flowed upward where Eagle/Condor watched with her higher self. Below her feet, animals supported her dancing and allowed her great happiness. Why, indeed, should she be a Shaman when she had the entire world at her command?

Then a bolt came from above, taking the colors out of her world and turning all pale green/blue. Without color, the reluctant Shaman had to hold herself in place. Her supports faltered. No more did she feel the loving eye of Eagle/Condor and higher self and the support of her animal friends, but rather the coldness of spheres and the rigidity of harsh planes.

She decided she must act. She took the sword that had pierced her world and transformed it into light energy that coalesced into crystals at her feet. The spheres above overturned, and light showered down over her body. A star shimmered above, its swirling light energy illuminating the Shaman's body as she flowed with ease into her soul's purpose. The end.

Rewrite the story using "I" as the main character. See how this moves your story. See where you need to shift at the mythic and energetic levels.

My story. Once upon a time, I was a reluctant Shaman. I had been at the center of the world, and everything I wanted flowed into me. Snake surrounded me, and my energy flowed upward where Eagle/Condor watched with my higher self. Below my feet, animals supported my dancing and allowed me great happiness. Why, indeed, should I be a Shaman when I had the entire world at my command?

Then a bolt came from above, taking the colors out of my world and turning all pale green/blue. Without color, I had to hold myself in place. My supports faltered. No more did I feel the loving eye of Eagle/Condor and higher self and the support of my animal friends, but rather the coldness of spheres and the rigidity of harsh planes.

I decided I must act. I took the sword that had pierced my world and transformed it into light energy that coalesced into crystals at my feet. The spheres above overturned, and light showered down over my body. A star shimmered above, its swirling light energy illuminating my body as I flowed with ease into my soul's purpose. The end.

As we move through the days, sometimes we disappoint ourselves and do not accomplish all we intend. Other days, we do more than we thought possible. We hold beliefs, which may not be our own but, rather, were given to us by a parent, relative, teacher, or friend. Those beliefs may limit our ability to grow and heal.

Sometimes, they create a back door. Back doors are ways out. "I can not do X, because _____." What are your limiting beliefs?

What stops you from doing "X"? How do you want your life to be different? What do you want? How do you want your life to be? What qualities do you want in your life? Take some time to really think about your values. Think about all the things that are truly important to you. Are you incorporating those important things into your daily life? Are you actually living the life you want to live?

For example: *I want to: breathe freely; be a healthy weight and eat good food; ride with a balanced and centered seat; play the harp well enough to perform publicly; develop my skills as a healer; develop my skills as a Shaman; communicate telepathically with animals; grow a community of like-minded healers who draw talented teachers to the place I live; continue to deepen the connection with my husband; care for my aging parents with grace and love; and learn to work with the Devas and Spirits of my land so the plants there thrive. I want to: share my abundance with my friends and wish for them the deep contentment and joy I find most days of my life if they desire this; continue to deepen my connection to the Earth; and have the resources to do all I want without compromise or guilt. I want to breathe freely.*

I want qualities of: calm, peace, joy, learning, growth, balance, expansion, introversion, and breath.

Go into Luminous Awareness. Remember to bring yourself into Luminous Awareness, leave your eyes open, look around, and see. I see . . . without judgment. Close your eyes. I hear. I smell. I taste. I sense (tactile sensing). Be aware of your breath. Use the 7-7-7 breathing meditation. When your eyes open, be aware they are the same eyes open or closed!

How have your limiting beliefs served you? They are familiar, easy, and safe. Fear of what will take their place is limiting. So, are these beliefs serving in a healthy way, or are they blocking? If I take this step, what happens? If I _____, then _____. Using word deconstruction, go into the three centers and levels of awareness. When in Eagle/Condor, go into the knowing of the Orb. At the level of Eagle/Condor, there is a place that occasionally appears out of nowhere. Although you can learn to see this place, it is difficult to describe in words. A little like a crystal ball, where pictures are very clear inside but what is inside cannot come out, I see this space as an Orb. There, you can see between what is there and go into the spaces between those things. See the spaces between things, like the spaces between these words, or the spaces between notes of music, or the space between your inhalation and your exhalation. Become aware of the connection between the spaces. See more spaces. From there, see the binding piece—that piece that holds you in place. Do not forget the process. Release forward motion. Be as a hummingbird at a feeder and hover. It can become easy to seek your own projections. Be clear about what is yours and what is <u>not</u> yours. We are often bound by the projections others have about us. When you step out of that co-dependent state, you can be aware of yourself. When you make a projection, make it a great one!

Create a Vision Statement by defining how you walk in the world and how you walk in all you do. Notice that the word "want" shows a lack of presence. Take this word "want" out. This has to do with your relationship with yourself. As you connect to that which is your center and the collective of your stones, you transform. As you transform, so does the world!

Exercise. This exercise needs to be done with a partner. First, one person recapitulates their life, taking no more than 45 minutes. This does not have to be chronological or linear. While speaking, go to places you may have blocked off or not wanted to revisit. The second person acts as a witness. As witness, stand back and really listen. If your partner says things that are limiting beliefs or seems stuck, say "I'm observing_____." Be a mirror so that the presenter can become aware of these places. Jot down those limiting beliefs so they may be added to the Nature Painting. Deconstruct them. You can now let anything that does not serve you die. You may want to tear up strips of paper to represent those limiting beliefs and put them in the painting to mulch and settle a little. As recorder, where there is still a charge, note it. This process is the death of stuff that no longer serves you. Get rid of the "I wish I had _____." Get rid of all the things you no longer wish to carry. Be aware. Be present.

Now that you have transformed your stories, your ancestors, and your roles, and you have reviewed your life and deconstructed any remaining blocks, stuck pieces, or "shoulds," you are ready to step on to the Shaman's Path. You are moving into a healed state. This healed state is one in which you are aware of how you walk and move in the world. You are ready to create a vision of the "new" you and to anchor this self to your current, revised, reality.

Exercise. First, create a vision statement. How do I walk? How do I move? How do I live? Your vision statement creates movement from the old map of projections to the new map of the healed state. What qualities do you want in all that you do? You may also want to do a vision board. What would be there now? See the new you emerge in your vision and then transform into reality in the fire! Create your vision board on a piece of wrapping paper and use this as the foundation for your Despacho. Cut out pictures of the things you are becoming or see yourself becoming and how you are now walking in the world. Draw your own little pictures or use words if that works better for you.

Go to your Nature Painting. Sit in Sacred Space. Open your Mesa at the eastern side of the painting, and, first, take the stones of the South. Hold each and honor it. Let love surround your stones and yourself. Place the stone onto the Mesa. As you add the second stone, gently tap it on the first. Repeat this process with the stones of the West, the North, and the East. At the end, you will have tapped the last stone 12 times. As you tap, create a welcoming greeting for each stone: "Welcome, dear friend, to my Mesa. Now you are part of the collective." Or, create a welcoming statement/intention for your stones. Finally, add your Lineage Stone. Tap it on the other stones in welcome. Close your Mesa. Then, create an Ayni Despacho with your vision board as its foundation. All you desire, all that you need to release to transform will then go to the fire in ceremony. The Despacho fire will transform the energy released in your Nature Painting as well as welcome your new stones, and your complete Healer's Mesa, to the collective.

In this work, as you move from one part of the wheel to the next, you transform. In each of those transformations is a "little" death. Death of the physical body is a different kind of transformation. A Despacho of transformation and beauty honors the "death" that was created by your intention to transform, in a very different, and, more specific, way. In moving to the Western way, you have transformed. Let the next Despacho you create be an "Aya" Despacho, a "Death" Despacho. This ceremony welcomes you into the new you, as a being walking the medicine path.

An Aya Despacho is also used to honor the spirit of the recently departed. After a ceremony, described below, which unwinds the chakras and loosens them from the physical body, freeing the spiritual body, an Aya Despacho creates a sense of connection and closure.

Death Rites

After someone has passed, clear his or her physical body so the person's spirit/soul/energy body can be free of the physical body. The chakra energy is unwound to free the soul from the body. Do this within 48 to 72 hours of death. Sooner is better. This can be done with the person's permission (or that of his/her family) either on the body's chakras, or on stones to represent the chakras from a distance.

1. Say a prayer for the deceased. Open your Wiracocha.

2. Start at the heart and loosen the field with your hand, a feather, or a rattle. Connect and be present.

3. Close to the body, in a counterclockwise direction using your rattle (or hand or feather), unwind the chakras and pull the energy out and upward. Each cycle is done separately, starting with the heart chakra and proceeding to the crown. Backwash (unscrew) the chakra until the energy flow is

smooth and easy. When you sense the chakra is clear, proceed to the next chakra. Backwashing of the chakras loosens the energy body. Begin at the heart center. Proceed as follows: heart to solar plexus; heart to solar plexus to throat; heart to solar plexus to throat to sacral; heart to solar plexus to throat to sacral to third eye; heart to solar plexus to throat to sacral to third eye to root; and then heart to solar plexus to throat to sacral to third eye to root to crown chakra. Before you move to a new chakra, always start at the heart.

4. Then, when all chakras are unwound, hold the feet and give a little nudge and think it done. Inform the energy body that "it is okay to go."

5. Once the energy body has left the physical body, seal all the chakras by placing a "+" (plus) using either Florida Water or essential oil, starting with the crown chakra and ending with the root chakra. This seals the chakras so spirit cannot return to a dead physical body.

(Note: The "unwinding" can be done on the living as a "high" cleansing. Do the unwinding a little further from the body and when done, rake the chakras with your hands and get the density out of the energy body. When done, rewind the chakras into the body with your hand, beginning at the crown and ending at the root.)

After the unwinding, an Aya Despacho can be created as a way to honor the entity's spirit and help it to move to the next realm. An

Aya Despacho is another way to lovingly assist a cherished family member or friend to die consciously. The ceremony provides deep celebration for the life of the individual who is in the process of, or has already, departed, and brings energetic closure to the physical body. The intention of the Despacho is to create a rainbow bridge between the worlds and to ease the process of crossing over for the loved one. As symbolic elements and prayers of gratitude are added, the Despacho comes alive with the energy of creation, and the essence of the person being celebrated and honored.

During an Aya Despacho ceremony, the Shaman works with the family and friends of the individual who is dying or already departed, encouraging them to share their prayers and reminiscences. The person's favorite food is served, favorite jokes told, and tears flow freely. Any unfinished business or remaining heavy energy is represented symbolically in the Aya Despacho. This heavy energy becomes food to send the beloved on his/her way across the rainbow bridge. The Aya Despacho process is very structured. You want to build separate layers to honor each of the worlds through which your loved one has traveled or will journey to in the future. The "old" you has, in essence, died. The new you, is stepping onto a new path. Honor the death of your "past," and welcome the birth of the new. Create an Aya Despacho, with joy for your newly healed self, to conclude this work.

The journey is now complete. Old stories no longer inform the present or help to influence the future. Ancestral strands of DNA no longer serving your highest good have been severed and the energy body made lighter. All the roles you used to play, and the various themes in your life, have been fully explored and traced back to both their beginning, and to their natural conclusion. You have honored the spirits of the place you were born and welcomed, with joy and love, the help of those where you now reside. Now, it is a time to walk forward in the healed state and share your true purpose with the world.

In right relationship with all that is, be, <u>now</u>, in joy.

PART TWO

TOOLS FOR HEALING

SIX

Working with Your Chakras

Considerable work has recently been published to help people to understand chakras and work with their own, as well as those of family, friends, and pets. If you are new to the chakra system, you will find a wealth of information both published and on-line. The focus here will be on how the chakras work with the Luminous Field, informing your vision, creating blocks, and otherwise either enhancing the flow of energy in your life, or conversely, slowing the flow and gumming things up.

The word "chakra" is Sanskrit and means, literally, "spinning disk." Those spinning disks contain patterns of energy from the time of the soul's creation to the present. They are very sensitive to our feelings and to the feelings of those around us. I view them as the body's first line of defense, both physically and emotionally. Awareness of the Luminous Field through the chakras, allows a clear and unbiased look at our emotions, our desires, and our back doors.

For many years, only the seven major chakras were discussed, and those seven do most of the work in the body. Recently, several other chakras have been "discovered" and are often worked with in various energy healing sessions, such as Reiki or Healing Touch. Chakras have also been identified on all 220 acupuncture meridians, and freeing blocks in those points is what helps to make acupuncture so effective.

When the chakras are "healthy," they spin quickly in a clockwise direction and are very colorful. The energy of this spin cleans our Luminous Field, our aura, and allows subtle communication with other beings wherever we go. When the chakras are blocked, the flow is blocked. The chakra might hold "dense" or "stuck" energy. The energy field then looks a little like that of the "Pigpen" character in Charles Schultz's "Peanuts." When the flow is blocked, often the areas related to that chakra in the physical body are also blocked. Basically, when a chakra is blocked, the physical body becomes much more susceptible to disease. The chakras hold our stories for us. They hold our hurts and sorrows, as well as our joys and desires. When those stories or hurts are removed from the chakra, both our physical body and our Luminous Body can flow into a healed state.

For the work done in this cosmology, I will talk about nine chakras and relate these to the three "worlds" and three "levels of awareness" in the Shaman's view. About two feet beneath our feet is the earthgate chakra. This chakra helps to ground our physical body in the Earth plane and directly connects us to Pachamama. I sense this chakra as a greenish brown with a smell like fresh, spring dirt. It is the only chakra with which I associate a smell. This connection to the belly of the Mother enters our physical body through the root/base chakra. The earthgate chakra is the ninth chakra. When you open your Wiracocha, you source from this point.

The root, the first chakra, is most often depicted as red in color. It moves straight down from between your legs, through the Earthgate chakra, connecting us to the center of the Earth. The root chakra grounds us to the physical. It relates to physical issues of the blood, bones, and muscles. The root activates at birth and helps us desire and search for a place of security (*i.e.*, food, clothing, shelter). It vibrates to the note of C and helps us to move confidently out into the world.

When our physical body is secure, it starts thinking about having a good time. It tickles the sacral chakra into learning to have fun. The sacral chakra can be found spinning on both the front and back of the body about two inches below the navel. It is generally depicted as orange in color and vibrates to the note of D. This chakra likes its pleasures and searches them out in sex, food, and other areas of creativity. When it is healthy, those areas of our lives are enriched and balanced. The sacral holds stories relating to our pleasure, as well as stories of abuse. The sacral governs the sexual organs in the physical body, as well as those organs relating to elimination of digested foods.

From a well-developed and cared for sacral chakra, a centered and thoughtful person can grow into their full power in the solar plexus chakra. This chakra, yellow in color and holding the vibration of the note of E, holds our will and sense of self. It is the place where our "gut" reactions take place. It is a place of "knowing" and "recognizing" what is good for us and what is not so good. The brain may be in the head, but the solar plexus is where one really thinks and puts oneself forward to the world. In my years as a Healing Touch practitioner, I have found, that for most people, either the sacral or the solar plexus chakra requires the deepest healing over time. These two chakras hold our ability to have fun and to reason. When we have that going for us, we are ready for love.

The fourth chakra, the heart, is the bridge of love connecting the lower vibrations of the Earthgate, root, sacral, and solar plexus, and the higher vibrations of the throat, third eye, crown chakra and transpersonal point. In the heart is Chocochinchi, Otorongo, Mother/Sister Jaguar. Emotions of love, anger, fear, and confusion all reside in the heart. This chakra encompasses the physical heart, the lungs, and the breasts, as well as the ability to nurture, to care, and to be empathetic. The heart, in my view, contains all that makes a living be-ing (and yes, animals, trees, plants, fish, and all things on the Earth, as well as the Earth itself are living be-ings of light and love). In the heart is love. The chakra is generally green, but can flash with streaks of rosy pink when love shines out, and it vibrates to the note of F, as well as to the lovely Sanskrit chant of Om. When this chakra is out of balance, most often one sees breast or lung cancer, heart disease, or respiratory afflictions in the physical. The songs that say "love is the answer" or "all we need is love, love," sum up the needs of the heart chakra very well.

When grounded and secure, able to have fun, confident in one's abilities, and able to love, all that wondrous emotion can be expressed through the throat. The throat chakra governs communication. A healthy throat chakra allows one to speak one's own truth, to stand up for one's beliefs, and to walk with purpose in the world. Light blue or silver in color, vibrating to the note of G, the throat chakra allows us to fully express ourselves to the world. The throat chakra connects the Middle World to the Upper World.

The third eye chakra, a deep indigo in color, vibrating to the note of A, allows one to see with the Shaman's sight. That sight is an awareness of the "other" that is there; a deep dreaming; and a connection to that sense of something "more" out there. When the Shaman journey's, she/he moves through the crown or third eye to fully experience the other levels of existence in the lower, middle and Upper Worlds. Here, Eagle/Condor sees everything in its big picture wholeness, and, here, one shifts from the mundane to the mythic. The third eye is the eye of Apuchin. The eye of the Eagle sees all that is without judgment or feeling.

The crown chakra, sitting like a lovely translucent purple or white bowl on the top of the head vibrating to the note of B, allows one to connect fully with the Divine. This is the chakra of spirituality and awareness of the cosmos. In spirit, that place from which we source, we accept new energy from Father Sky, Grandmother Moon, and the Star Nations and recognize our connection to "all that is." From that place, we can become aware of our transpersonal place, the stargate or transpersonal point. The stargate chakra can be found just above your head. You will find your eighth chakra by raising your hand over your head and turning your palm toward the sky. Generally, the chakra will be right there and drop into your hand. This is also the point to which you go when opening your Wiracocha.

Your transpersonal point also holds all the other chakras in place, both before birth and after death. The transpersonal point, gathers the energy and stories of the all the other chakras at death, and is the light of the soul. From the eighth chakra, you "POOF," giving up whatever is needed up to the Universe.

There are many books, classes, workshops, and methods for working with chakras and helping them to heal. In all, *intention* is the key. One of the simplest methods on this path to work with your chakras is to use the Shamanic journey. Set your intention to journey to the Lower World to meet spirit guides or medicine people, and ask for healing. Ask the Gatekeeper to help you to rebalance and heal your chakras. Call spirit guides with whom you have worked to come to you and perform a healing. Be aware of shifts in your physical body as you journey.

When you return, gently hold each chakra in your dominant hand. Ask that it continue to heal and to function at a level for your best and highest good. Then, hold your hands, palms up, in front of you and ask that your hands be filled with any colors or energies you need at this moment. When your hands feel full, intuitively place them on your body, wherever you feel called to do so, for a few moments and intend the healing energy to create balance in your energy body and your physical body.

Healthy chakras help to create both healthy energetic and physical bodies. Clogged, dirty, or blocked chakras are not able to create the balance needed to maintain health in the physical. Blocks in chakras can be "caused" by many things. Some of these are as simple as being around someone with an "attitude" that does not bring you joy. Some are caused by a past life issue. Some are caused by one's own beliefs. Some are caused by the projections of others. Some are caused by physical or emotional abuse. Many of these issues may require counseling, and the practices in this book will not provide a "cure." However, as an adjunct to other modalities and ways of seeing the world, clearing blocks in the chakras helps speed up the process of healing.

On this path, many of our stories and issues have been given up to our Kuyas and now reside in our Mesa. But, to remove those stories from our energy field, they need to be removed from the chakra holding the energy of that story. To find the "culprit" chakra, it is necessary to learn how to determine which chakra is blocked and holding that stuck energy. The "culprit" chakra will be discharging or sending energy about that subject in a counter-clockwise direction.

In other modalities, the overall "spin" of each chakra is measured. Chakras can spin in various directions. They might not spin at all. Basically, with most forms of energy work on chakras, a healthy chakra spins clockwise. An unhealthy chakra spins in some other way (horizontally, elliptically, counterclockwise, vertically, etc.). However, in this cosmology, we are not inquiring about the overall health of a chakra. Our intention is to ask which chakra is holding the stuck energy. That chakra will always be discharging the energy in a counterclockwise pattern. Sometimes more than one chakra is holding the stuck energy. In this work, when you clear the lowest chakra, all the others will line up and the energy will flow freely. Always clear the lowest discharging chakra first, and then recheck the field to ensure the work is complete.

Using a Pendulum

The fastest way to see the spin of a chakra is to hold a pendulum over the area of the chakra and ask a question about that chakra's spin. You can ask that you see how the chakra is spinning generally.

You can ask if the chakra is holding a specific issue. You can ask for the overall health or energy pattern of the chakra. Remember, for the work done in this cosmology, your question is simple: "Which chakra is holding the stuck energy regarding 'X' problem?" Your clear intention allows the pendulum to provide the answer you need to continue.

Pendulums are as varied as the people who use them. They can be quite elegant and made of various kinds of crystals, or they can be designed for dowsing and made of bronze or copper. They can also be as simple as a lifesaver on a string or piece of dental floss. In a pinch, I have used my key ring. Anything that dangles and can move in a circular way will work. When using a pendulum made of any kind of crystal, be aware that the crystal can have an impact on the chakra. That is their nature and one of their roles as we use them. With a crystal pendulum, include in your intent that the crystal not influence the chakra's spin. Also, be aware that the crystal may take on some of the chakra 's stuck energy. Clear your crystal pendulum often by spritzing it with Florida Water.

As with any skill, practice makes perfect. Pendulums can be used to answer most "yes" or "no" questions. Some like to give "yes" answers by swinging vertically, like someone nodding their head up and down. Some prefer to circle clockwise for "yes." Some like to answer "no" by swinging sideways like a person shaking their head "no." Some will circle counter-clockwise. So, to begin ask your pendulum for a "yes." Ask your pendulum for a "no." Test these answers with simple questions. For example:

"My name is _____."

"My address is _____ "

"My mother's name is _____."

"I was born in the city of _____."

You should get a "yes" answer when you insert the right answer in the blank and a "no" answer when you deliberately say something untrue. This work helps to calibrate your pendulum. It also helps you to gain confidence that the pendulum is giving you the "right" answer. Sometimes, I doubt my pendulum and myself. When that happens, I call a friend and ask her to check with her pendulum. All I have to say is: "Please ask your pendulum if the answer to my question is 'yes'." I do not have to explain the problem (sometimes one asks very personal questions of one's pendulum). I just want independent verification. So when in doubt, ask a friend. Over time, and with practice, you will come to trust in your pendulum.

To measure the chakras, hold the pendulum over the chakra you wish to measure and ask your pendulum to show you how it is spinning. You may get a clockwise spin going very quickly and very large. Or the spin could be slow and the circle small. The pendulum could move elliptically, up and down, sideways, or be still. All that one needs to know for most energy work is that chakras are either open or blocked. If they are open the pendulum will spin clockwise. If the chakra is blocked the pendulum will spin some other way (or not at all). Be aware that any other way a chakra spins really does not matter. The block needs to be removed so the chakra's energy can flow. However, that is a different kind of energy work. The intention in the Shaman's work is simply: "Which chakra is holding this issue?" That chakra will spin in a counterclockwise direction whether or not it is otherwise fairly healthy and balanced or not.

Over time, you may learn to feel the individual energy field of each chakra. You may learn to use a tuning fork or other kind of chime to hear the vibration. There are many other ways to determine if a chakra is blocked. However, start to work with a simple pendulum. They work really well for determining which chakras need to be cleared when doing this work.

Exercise. A Chakra Meditation. Read through the entire exercise before you begin and plan to spend as much time as you feel is needed at each chakra. To begin, sit quietly with your spine erect and your feet flat on the floor, hands relaxing palms up in your lap. Practice the 7-7-7 breathing exercise, and deeply relax. Then, take two or three deep cleansing breaths in through your nose and out through your mouth. Feel a connection to the Earth through your feet. Feel the support of your chair. Allow your head to float above your neck and be relaxed.

Bring your attention to the earthgate chakra two feet below the ground between your feet. Slowly raise your dominant hand from your lap and turn the palm toward the chakra. Imagine that you are holding the top of the chakra like it is a large ball of the Earth. Your hand can move slowly in a clockwise direction over the ball, enhancing the chakra's spin. Gently spin the chakra and become aware of its shape, size, and energy. Take between five and nine breaths with each chakra to really feel that center. Then turn your palm toward the root chakra between your legs.

The root chakra travels like a column of light between your legs and grounds you to the Earth. Feel the warmth of the chakra as you find its shape and imagine its strength as it spins to support your physical body on Earth. Move your hand to the sacral chakra. Be aware of its orange energy. Again, gently spin the chakra and become aware of its shape, size, and its creative power. Breathe into this energy. Breathe with this energy.

Your hand moves to the solar plexus chakra, above your navel. It warms your hand like sunshine on a spring day. Breathe into this center and be at one with the power of your own self. You have a right to your own space, and here it is in the solar plexus chakra. Gently spin the solar plexus chakra in a clockwise direction. Feel its energy move into your palm. Feel the powerful strength of this chakra as you become aware of your own strength and power. As your palm moves to your heart, a wave of love and joy washes over your entire body. Your heart accepts the love from the other chakras. It feels the energy that has poured into your hands and welcomes the lower chakra energies in the heart center. The heart pulses rays of love back into your palm, sending love through your entire body.

Your hand moves to rest just above your throat, and the blue and silver energy of that chakra vibrates with joy as it experiences the love received from your heart. Breathe in this gentle light. Gently spin your throat chakra in a clockwise direction. Feel the vibration of song and creativity move into your palm. Feel the expression of the throat. Your palm now moves over your third eye, and images of swirling indigo light come into your view. The colors merge and swirl and fill your hand with energy. Feel the energy as you use your hand to gently spin the chakra. When your palm turns to your crown, a sense of deep peace permeates every cell of your being. You are home. You are loved. You are part of the Universe, and the crown chakra opens and accepts these gifts from heaven. Here, feel the clockwise spin of your crown and welcome the peace now surrounding your physical body.

As your palm rises above your head and reaches for the sky, your eighth chakra, the transpersonal point, falls into your outstretched palm. Here, the energy of all the chakras is balanced and held in harmony. Hold this point and be aware that as your arm tires, you notice that your other palm has filled with the colors of all your chakras. You are holding a swirling ball of colors in your hand. Bring that palm to your heart, and cover it with your other hand. Take a few deep breaths as the colors move to their home chakra and balance them. You become aware of the love and joy the Universe is offering to you as each chakra is balanced.

When you feel the exercise is complete, let your palms fall again to your lap. Breathe deeply. Become aware of your feet on the floor. Be aware of your body. Just sit and be for a few moments. In harmony and completely balanced, you are now ready to begin to assemble your day.

SEVEN

Care and Feeding of
Your Mesa and Power Animals

The Mesa

When I began this journey, my first teacher said to find three
stones that gave me joy. I was told to wrap them in a small and
pretty piece of cloth to keep them safe and together. The stones
should not be too big. They should be small enough to easily hold
or to travel with or to put in my pocket. I was not given very good
advice because there was not enough information for me to know
what these stones were going to do, how I would use them, or, how
they would help me grow.

As you pick stones to use in your healing journey, choose
stones that give you joy. Know that you will be traveling with
them. Indeed, they will go many places with you. They may sleep
with you; go hiking with you; travel on an airplane, or by train, or
bus. They will help you do healing work with yourself and with
others. They will assist you when you journey and help you find
answers to many of life's deeper questions. You will eventually
have nine to 13 stones, or sometimes a few more, in your bundle. A
cloth that is large enough to hold that many stones is needed. The
usual dimension is 22" x 24" or almost square. The stones will not
fit in your pocket!

Choosing the cloth that holds your stones is almost as important as choosing the stones themselves. Many people create little mini-quilts to hold their stones. The quilt can be lined with another pretty cloth that the stones are first wrapped in and then placed in the larger cloth, called a *Mestana*. The *Mestana,* or Mesa cloth, holds the stones and is the foundation of the traveling altar the Mesa represents.

Your Mesa becomes a sacred medicine bundle that represents all you were, all you are, and all of who you are be-coming. If you wrap it up and put it on a shelf, over time, you forget what the stones represent. You forget why they are important. You forget how they can help and guide you.

However, the stones do not forget you. Your Mesa holds you. It holds you in love and supports your walk on the Earth. For this great service, it asks very little in return other than to be recognized and fed by you. Open your Mesa on Saturday night, and feed it with corn meal or tobacco or a spritz of Florida Water. Arrange the stones and let them commune with others around the world. Take your Mesa with you into nature. Go on a hike, and when you take a break, open it and spread the stones around you. Meditate. Ask the stones to tell you of their travels. Ask them to increase your awareness. Be aware of their strong presence as individuals.

Create ceremony. Open your Mesa. Arrange your stones around the edge of your *Mestana*, and create a Despacho in the center of it. Close the Despacho and press the Despacho to your heart chakra and then to all your chakras. Press your Mesa to the Despacho. Imprint your prayers on your energy field with your Mesa through the Despacho. The exception to imprinting with the Despacho is the Kutti Despacho. A Kutti Despacho is designed to remove negative energy from your field. The negativity goes into the Despacho and is burned with an Ayni Despacho. You do not want to imprint that negativity back into your Mesa or your Luminous Body.

Take your Mesa with you to bed at night. Open it next to the place you sleep and ask the stones to guide your dreamtime. Or, leave it in its bundle and put it under your pillow to help protect you on your nightly travels. Use your Mesa as a pillow when you lie down to journey or meditate. Talk with your Mesa.

As I am typing this, I notice that my Mesa is resting in its usual place on a nearby drum. As my awareness increases, I hear that it would like to sit on my lap so it can help me write!

Working with Power Animals

Working with power animals is another much discussed and written about New Age topic. Learning I work with power animals, people often tell me what specific animal just crossed their path and ask: "What does that mean?" Frankly, those kinds of incidences mean whatever you want them to mean. The power of the animal is what it can tell you based upon your beliefs and knowledge about that animal's habits. However, until you are comfortable with power animals, it is very useful to have a reference guide handy. *Animal Speak* by Ted Andrews is one of the most definitive.

Shamanic practitioners are best known for two kinds of major healing techniques: soul retrieval (which is beyond the scope of this book), and power animal retrieval. When a person is ill, they have lost some of their own power. The reasons for that are many, but, often, a lack of power means the animals that were working with that individual have abandoned him/her and a new animal helper needs to be found.

When humans are born, an animal or two agrees to take on guardianship of that individual and to help the person throughout the person's life on Earth. Most of the time, people are unaware of this help, do not acknowledge it, and often think it a "most ridiculous" idea. If you have read that far in this book, it may be time for you to start thinking more seriously about your power animals and how you want to work with them.

Some animals come with us at birth. If they leave, we lose our power. Other animals come to us at various times in our lives when we need or ask for their help. Finding your animal is not hard, but it is not an easy process either. If you have always had a love of a particular kind of wild animal, there is a good chance that one is also your power animal. Dogs, cats, cows, pigs, and other domesticated animals are usually not power animals. In my view, these animals have taken on too much human baggage and too many human problems, and need power animals of their own to return them to power. However, if you have always had an affinity for blue birds, for example, and notice them often, or you are always drawn to the giraffe exhibit at the zoo, one of these may be your power animal. Do you have a collection of frogs, owls, elephants, or horses? That is a clue, too!

If you haven't given much thought to animals up until now, pay attention to those crossing your path. You will be surprised to discover the variety of birds and wild animals inhabiting most city streets. If you are lucky enough to live near the country, you may start becoming aware of animals you had not noticed before. Awareness of who else is around you provides the first real clue.

And, although it may be exciting to work with lions and tigers and bears, there is much to be gained from working with other animals, including mice, foxes, and salmon. Each being offers a unique perspective and unique characteristics and gifts. The view the mouse has of the Earth is much different than the view of the elephant or lion. The view of the owl is different than that of the salmon. Start to notice the animals and birds you see and meditate about what that sighting may have to tell you. Or, journey with that animal and ask it to tell you more about itself.

When noticing animals, begin first to bring them to awareness. For example, in the winter, where I live, there is are red-tailed hawks sitting on fence posts along every highway. Sometimes, the hawks are sitting up in trees. It is a common sight. Sometimes, on a short drive, one could see as many as 15 hawks just hanging out. Those hawks are not offering much of a message. However, when you go out to do ceremony and open space to the East and ask for Eagle/Condor/Apuchin to fly high over your space and a hawk appears out of the East and flies over your space as the words come out of your mouth, well, that bird has something special to tell you.

Animals are available to offer advice, to help one to travel to the Lower World, to help with healings, or to provide answers to other kinds of questions. Often, however, their messages are written in symbols and signs that modern humans no longer know how to read. Trained by the modern education system to be logical and to make decisions based on facts and figures, reading the signs given by an animal lead many people running to a book or the internet for an answer. And, there is some value in getting ideas about what various animals may be appearing in your life from these sources. However, do not assume that what you read about an animal is the entire message. What the animal is actually trying to tell you may not be at all related to someone else's interpretation. Take the time to really get to know the animal's way of living in the world.

First, identify an animal with which you have an affinity. Find out all you can about that animal. Where does it usually live? Is it a hunter? Is it prey? What does it like to eat? What does it do during the day? What does it do at night? Does it hide? Does it live in a cave? Is it quiet and shy, or outgoing and noisy? Does it live alone or with a family? All these are clues to the messages you might receive. Ask your pendulum, is "x" my power animal? When you discover your power animal, take a journey with the intent of meeting your individual power animal. Animals live in a collective unit, but those who work with people usually come and hang out with us and are waiting for us to visit in the Lower World. Journey. Go down, down. Cleanse yourself in the pool. Ask Huascar if you may enter. Ask Huascar to help you find your power animal. Call to the animal. When your animal finds you, both of you will react with joy! Travel together for a while. Then, if you can, promise to come back often to learn more about each other.

If you still have no idea which animal may be your power animal, or if you feel your power animal may have abandoned you, journey to find a new animal.

Journey. Journey with the intent of finding a new power animal. Open Sacred Space. Open your Wiracocha. Go to the place in nature that you usually go to journey in the Lower World. Go down, down. Cleanse yourself in the pool. Ask Huascar if you may enter. Ask Huascar to help you find your power animal. As you travel, you will see many animals. Generally, an animal you see for the third time is likely to be your power animal. On the third siting, ask: "Are you my power animal?" When you get a "yes," ask: "Will you come back with me to my world and help me?" Or, you may see groups of the same kind of animal. If so, ask generally of the group if one of them is your power animal. If the answer is yes, ask if one of them will come back with you. Either way, when you have that "yes" from a specific animal, gather the animal into your heart and come back. Welcome this new animal to your life with ceremony. Create a Despacho in honor of this new relationship.

Create a little altar in honor of your power animal. Collect statues or pictures. Place these together in a scared space and when you journey offer your prayers and love to this spiritual helper. Dance as if you were your animal. Cry out as if you were that animal. If you are so inclined, add a tattoo of the animal somewhere on your body. Be playful and accepting of this new relationship, as you welcome this new being into your life.

Let the animal's spirit flow throughout your body. Know that you are not alone.

EIGHT

Sacred Ceremony

In this work, creating ceremonies is essential for the transformation from the mundane to the mythic. The ceremony is the vehicle that takes one to spirit and allows transformation to begin. Ceremony can be as simple as a lighting a candle with intent, lighting a small fire and making an offering, smudging one's self or one's space with smoke (generally sage or incense), or as elaborate as a Despacho. When in doubt about what to do, create ceremony.

A few ideas for simple ceremony follow. Use your imagination to enhance and expand these steps and let the spirit of the ceremony move you to a place of new awareness.

For example, let us say you have some sort of nagging problem. You are unsure what to do, in which direction to turn, where to start. Do ceremony. Write your problem on a piece of paper. Add the potential solutions. Fold the paper, and hold it next to your heart. Breathe for a few moments just letting the energy of your heart flow into the problem written on the paper. Take the paper to a small fire. Offer some sage or tobacco or corn meal to the fire. Then send the paper to the fire asking that the solution be revealed to you at the appropriate time and that you will all of a sudden be aware of what you need to do. Then let it go. The Universe will let you know what to do and when.

Or, you just received really good news. You are so happy and full of joy. Do ceremony. Gather incense and a few candles. Offer your prayers of gratitude and love to the candles and incense as you light them. Sit in the glow of the candles, and wash yourself in the smoke of the incense. Be present with spirit as your chakras rebalance with this new vibration of joy.

Some experiences seem to require a more formal ceremony (*e.g.*, graduations, weddings, and funerals are all ceremonies of this type). Sometimes, it is nice to offer gifts to your land for no reason at all but that you wish to be in right relationship, in Ayni, with your land. Sometimes, you wish to remove negative vibrations or the energies of negative people from your life (a bad boss or job or a broken and unhealthy relationship are two good examples). Sometimes, you would like to honor the dead or dying. Sometimes, you do not know what to do, but feel that a big ceremony will allow your spirit to open to the answer. For those occasions, create a Despacho. Despachos can be created for numerous intents including to make rain, to give strength to the land, to honor a marriage, or to honor a birth. The intent of the Despacho determines the ingredients you use. I like to begin all such "big" ceremonies in sacred and clear space.

Space Clearing

There are many reasons to clear your space on a regular basis, and it is a good practice to clear the space every time you clean it. So, first, clean house. At the very least, clean the room in which you are creating your Despacho. When the space is physically clean, go into each room and, in a counterclockwise direction, clap your hands, beat a drum, or rattle the old, stuck energy out. Then, using incense, sage, sweet grass, or cedar, fill the space with smoke. Move the smoke in a clockwise direction around each room. Use a feather or your breath to move the smoke into the corners to clear any remaining stuck energies from every nook and cranny. Smudging blesses the space as it also clears. Your intention of creating clear, loving space informs the smoke. Move the smoke behind the doors and into the closets. Just remember when you clear space to make sure a window is open so unwanted energies can leave. Camay (Ka-mai) is the breath, and with fire it is transformation. Your space will feel more than clean when it has also been cleared and blessed with smudging.

Sometimes, space requires a fire cleansing to clear all negativity from the space. For example, suppose a huge family argument took place in the dining room. Many words were spoken that have caused hurt feelings. Whenever anyone goes into that room now, you notice that those feelings of hurt and anger come to the surface. For a fire clearing, you will need: a small metal pan (like a cat food or tuna fish tin, or a small aluminum pie pan), Epsom salt, rubbing alcohol, matches, and a glass or porcelain plate. Cover the bottom of the pan with Epsom salt. A tablespoon or two should be plenty. Cover the salt with rubbing alcohol. Again, not too much is needed. Place the pan on the plate. Place the plate on a flat, clutter-free surface in the center of the room. Light a match and toss it into the alcohol.

The fire will burn brightly blue and only last for a few moments. While it burns, you can either stand quietly and observe, or you can talk "out" what you want to leave. Just say what you need to say to eliminate all the negativity from the space. When the fire stops burning spend a minute or two and send your love to the space. Say aloud what kind of energy you would like the room to hold. If you are so guided, you can write a prayer for the space and read it in each room as you clear it.

I once had two dogs that loved to bark at the front door whenever someone came by. I would yell and holler at the dogs, and generally work myself into a dither about the racket. I did not like my shouting any more than I liked the barking. I did a clearing to remove all the pent up negative energies created by my yelling. I opened my heart and sent loving energy to the foyer. I lit some sage and smudged the space with the intention of creating a quiet and calm entrance. I had to repeat this ceremony twice more, but eventually my dogs learned to be quiet when guests arrived, and I was no longer angry.

The traditional way in this cosmology of honoring the spirit of your land is to create an Ayni Despacho. This gift is offered whenever the spirit moves or at each solstice and equinox, and at each full moon. The Despacho can be small or large, depending on your intent and how you are structuring your ceremony.

Building a Ceremonial Fire

To build a ceremonial fire, begin with four or five pieces of tightly rolled newspaper. Place these in the bottom of the fire pit and layer small twigs in a tipi shape over the sides and top of the paper. Gradually add bigger sticks and finally a few logs. Do not use fire starters, chemicals, or chemically treated or painted wood/ lumber when making ceremonial fires. All materials should be from nature. Open Sacred Space around the fire pit and then light the newspaper in three or four places. Rattle and sing. Invite the organizing spirits of the Andes, as well as Everest, Mt. Shasta, Mt. Rainier, and local places, to your fire.

In the tradition of the high Andes, the mountain spirits, the Apus, are called in order after calling Pachamama, and then other sacred sites are called. Sing to them first in this order, and then call in other spirits from other sacred places in your area or places that you know (*e.g.*, the Mississippi River, Stonehenge, Lake Michigan, the Ozarks . . . there are a lot of places to name) or local sacred places. The ceremony awakens the place. The names to call are: Pachamama, Ausangate, Salcantay, Pacha Tucson, Everest, Huaca Wilka, Mama Simone, Machu Picchu, Huayna Picchu, Manuel Pinto, Yanantin, Mt. Rainier, Mt. Shasta, San Boleyn, Santa Warmi, Killia Wasi, Pancha Kollya, Mama Killia, Mama Cocha, Amaru, Chocochinchi, and Apuchin. However, do not worry if you forget any of these names, or welcome them in a different order. Your welcoming intention is all that matters. All that does matter is that you are doing ceremony to honor the spirits of your land.

Here is a song that can be chanted in English to call the Spirits of the Earth, Sea, and Air, to your fire:

"*Name of the spirit*" (Ausangate, Amaru, Stone People, etc.), *hear me calling.*

Awaken now and hear my call.

Here my gifts of love will feed you.

Loving light now surrounds us all.

In Quechan (for which there is no translation):

"Name of the spirit" Murayah kumu pai sita kayaya;

Si sai punti mariri; Kaya punti mariri.

("Name of the spirit" moor-ah-yah koo-moo pa see-ta kye-aye-aye-aye;

See sigh poon-tee ma-eer-ee-ee-ee; kye-aye poon-tee ma-eer-ee)

Continue with your chanting, using a different spirit's name each time. The song becomes a mantra. Spirit will know whichever song you sing or chant. You can find your own song! Invite the spirits to your fire ceremony. Sing other songs you know of welcoming and love. Know that Spirit enjoys your singing. Spirit also likes American folk songs like *Amazing Grace,* or *Swing Low, Sweet Chariot,* for example. Christmas carols during the holiday season are fine. Indeed, whatever songs spirit urge you to sing, sing to your fire. Sing, and as you sing, rattle in rhythm.

Song to the Apus

Lorie Allen

Pa-cha-ma-ma Mur-a-yah Ku-mu pai si-ta ka-ya-a-a si

sai pun-ti mar-i-ri (ee-ee) Ka-ya pun-ti mar-i-ri

Pachamama murayah kumu pai sita kayaya;
Si sai punti marii; Kaya punta mariri.

Pachamama
Ausangate
Salcantay
Pacha Tucson
Everest
Huaca Wilka
Mama Simone
Machu Picchu
Huayna Picchu
Manuel Pinto
Yanantin
Mt. Rainier
Mt. Shasta
Mt. Hood
San Boleyn
Santa Warmi
Killia Wasi
Pancha Kollya
Mama Killia
Mama Chocha
Amaru
Chocochinchi
Apuchin
Other spirts as moved

Pachamama Song

Lorie Allen

Pa-cha-ma-ma   mu-chan-a-pi   Yuar-in-chis-chi   ma-ma-ta-

ta   Was-in-chis-ta   ay-llun-chis-ta   Mun-as-kay-puan   kau-say-nin-chis-

pan

Pachamama muchanapi
Yuyarinchischi mamatayta
Wasinchista, ayllunchista
Munaskaypuan kausayninchispan

Pachamama hear me calling,
Shimmer here atop the sky.
Shimmer here beneath the ocean,
Warm your hands here at our fire.

Ausangate hear me calling,
The deep, green doorway opens here.
Over rocks, through clouds, and sunshine,
Strength we need here at the fire

Huaca Wilka hear me calling,
Your large smile lights the sky.
Down the stairway, in the sunshine,
Warm your body by our fire.

Mama Killia hear me calling,
Softly light our path tonight.
Be here, hold me gently,
At the fire here tonight

Apus, Apus, hear me calling.
Surround my space with your strong hands.
Prayer here and love will feed you.
Waken now from your deep slumber
Welcome, Welcome Angelic Beings!!

As you chant, the fire will become "friendly." The small twigs will ignite the sticks, and eventually the logs will fall to the center (you may need a poker to help you) and gently turn into glowing coals. You will know when the moment is right to offer your gift.

- Place a gift in the fire (*e.g.*, tobacco, a flower, a stick, whatever you have to offer).

- Release: Bring the fire into your belly with your breath and hands to cleanse and release that center. Unwind it in a counter-clockwise motion and push/blow it into the fire. These are affinity receptors attached to what you released that need to be cleansed. Do this at all three centers of exchange (Yachay, Munay, Llankay).

- Balance: Bring fire into the center and hold it there to balance. Repeat this at all three centers of exchange.

- Imprint. This third part is the most important, imprinting. You must be available. Bring the fire in with your breath and hands. Wind it into your centers of exchange in a clockwise manner. Imprint that center with fire and light.

- Use a little fire/smoke to wash and feed your Luminous Body.

- Take your Mesa to the fire and feed it by holding it over the fire and moving it upward in a clockwise spiral, making seven turns.

- If you are also offering a Despacho, place your final prayers into this offering and place it in the fire. Spirit has asked that Despachos be placed into the fire when the coals are burning steadily and with less smoke. Turn your back and slowly walk away as the Spirits come to consume your gift.

In 20 to 30 minutes, check to be sure your fire is out or in a safe place to continue burning. Do not extinguish this fire with water or other artificial means unless there is a danger of it spreading. Be sure you have time to maintain a watchful eye on your fire, do not do fire ceremonies on windy days, or days when the risk of fire is high. Gifts and Despachos can also be buried in ceremony following similar steps. Bury your offering when it is not safe to have fire.

Native American Fire Ceremony Song

To make the fire "friendly" and call upon the spirit of the waters beneath the Earth:

Nitche Tai tai, N U Y
Oro Nika Oro Nika
Hey Hey . . . . Hey Hey
Ooo Ai

Its essence:

O Great Mother, Mother of the Waters
We call on you, waters of our birth
Waters of our sustenance

Waters that cleanse us on our death
Waters of life.

Through the process of working with your stones, you have
moved to a place where you are no longer held by your stories. After
you wake each day, assemble your day: Dream your day into being
with stillness, prayer, and appreciation. Think about the progression
of release as you create meaning in almost everything you do.
Follow the energy. Do not fall back into the story. Follow the energy.

Creating the process without interference with an open heart
is the definition of *holding the space*. Holding space allows you to
shift into ceremony. Shifting into different perceptual states allows
you to walk the way of the Shaman. Taking your issues to the fire
in ceremony moves you to the mythic and sacred.

Ayni Despacho Ceremony

Despachos are created for many purposes, but most often
they are designed to help move the creator (person or group) into
a state of "right relationship" with the land, the water, or spirit.
Kits, containing all ingredients, can be obtained on-line from
several sources (see *Resources* at the end of the book). However,
Despacho ingredients are fairly easy to obtain and easily can be
adapted to local areas. Although the kits you can buy made in Peru
are fun and interesting, it honors the land to use local ingredients
and flowers. The list of ingredients is easily modified. Feel free to
add or subtract as the occasion demands and as special things, like

charms, are found. With every ingredient you add, breathe your intent into the item and place it with love.

All Despacho ceremonies include prayers that move through the Lower, Middle, and Upper Worlds and they are a beautiful creation of love and prayers. Of the ingredients noted in the following list, use what can be found, what speaks to the purpose of your ceremony, and what is on hand. Many people I know have a basket or tub full of their Despacho supplies so a ceremony may be created quickly when needed.

AYNI DESPACHO CEREMONY
INGREDIENT LIST

Ingredients are listed in the usual order in which they are added to the Despacho. In parentheses is noted what each item represents. Hold each item and inform it with your prayers and your intent.

- ❖ A piece of wrapping paper to hold the Despacho
- ❖ A bouquet of flowers, including red and white carnations
- ❖ 9 perfect bay leaves (per person participating in the ceremony) (to create Quintus to hold each person's prayers)
- ❖ Llama fat (butter, margarine, or Crisco, or beef, pork, or buffalo fat are substitutes) (to help the Despacho burn and connect Mother Earth to the Apus in each Quintu)
- ❖ Shell (the container, holding all the prayers)
- ❖ Sugar (sweetness)
- ❖ Candy doll or small doll (the creator of the Despacho, yourself or your group)
- ❖ Rice (fertility)
- ❖ Peanuts (the plant people)
- ❖ Lima Beans (sacred places in the land)
- ❖ Corn (fertility and growth, the tears of the sun)
- ❖ Tobacco (the sacred messenger)
- ❖ Garbanzo beans (the ancestors)
- ❖ Red and White Carnations (red for the Mother Earth, white for the Apus)
- ❖ Raisins (the ancestors)
- ❖ Lavender (calls the land spirits)
- ❖ 1 Dried Fig (the spirits of the mountains and all ancestors of the land)

- ❖ A piece of jerky (that which is yet unborn)
- ❖ Chocolate (to honor Pachamama)
- ❖ Magnetite/Mica/Silica—a piece of one of these (connects the Despacho to this land)
- ❖ Amaranth or anise seeds or Quinoa (growth and vitality)
- ❖ Little figurines of houses, cards, keys (important things in daily life)
- ❖ Animal crackers (four-legged friends)
- ❖ Candy figurines (the winged ones, angels, the upper states of consciousness)
- ❖ A Starfish (the heavens)
- ❖ Candied Stars and Fruits (life, goodness, fruition)
- ❖ 1 Round whole Cracker (wholeness and unity)
- ❖ A square of cotton fluff (the clouds)
- ❖ Sun and Moon Sequins (the astral bodies of the sun and the moon)
- ❖ Silver and Gold Rods (music)
- ❖ 2 small candles (any color except black, light the way to Heaven)
- ❖ A feather (so your gift flies to the sky)
- ❖ Rainbow Yarn (the rainbow bridge)
- ❖ Candy Stars (the star nations)
- ❖ Sage (to smell good, sacredness)
- ❖ More flowers (for beauty and to honor the plant kingdom)
- ❖ Incense (to smell good)
- ❖ Aromatic dough or cookies (sweetness)
- ❖ Stars or Sprinkles of many colors (celebration)
- ❖ A Bell (calls the spirits to the Despacho)
- ❖ Red Wine for Mother Earth
- ❖ White Wine for the Apus

❖ One whole red carnation and one whole white carnation (to sprinkle the wine)

❖ A ribbon to tie the package and hold it together

Begin your ceremony with a beautiful square of wrapping paper. Fold it up one-third and down one-third. Then fold it from the left one-third and the right one-third. When you open the paper there are nine lovely squares. The center square will receive your "ingredients." Or, fold your paper in half and then in half again, making a square. Beginning at the corner where the folds all meet, turn the paper in about one inch. Keep folding the paper six more times, for a total of seven turns, representing the seven primary chakras. When you open the paper, a diamond pattern emerges. Sprinkle a little sugar around the center of the paper. Place a shell in the middle of the paper. The shell will hold all your prayers in sweetness.

Next, gather beautiful bay leaves and create your Quintus. A Quintu is a group of three perfect bay leaves arranged as a fan to represent the three levels, three worlds, and three Earth archetypes. Include at least three Quintus, but you can create as many more as spirit directs. Place the three leaves together face up and place a little fat on the stems to hold them together. In Peru, llama fat is used. In North America, a little butter, margarine, or Crisco works just as well. Place a red flower petal on the stems to represent Mother Earth. Place a white flower petal on top of the red to represent the mountain spirits. Fill the Quintu with your prayers. Surround your prayers with love. Your prayers can be for fertility and Ayni (reciprocity), healing and light. Your prayers can be to release the past, embrace the present, and move into the future in Ayni. Your prayers are for you, and will change with each ceremony. Infuse them with your intent. Use your breath to move your prayers into your Quintus.

Use your breath to inform all the Despacho ingredients of your intent and blessings. "Sweet Mother, I want your hands to bless my heart to take away the pain of the land of my loved ones . . . Call others. May your light penetrate into the deepest crevice of my life and give me the clarity I need to change." Prayer is a dialog. Speak to God, to the Sun, to the Moon, to the Earth. Speak out loud. How can Pachamama hear you if you just think your prayers to yourself? Pray into each Quintu. Pour your love, your blessings, and your wishes into the prayer. Use your breath to inform them. Your Quintus release your intent to the Universe. They create a new guiding mythology and can even impact past lives.

If you are working with a Shaman who can read the bay leaves, he or she will imprint the leaves with their prayers and breath and toss them on a blanket prior to creating the Quintus. This process is repeated three times. Some of the reading may pertain to the entire group or class. Other parts may speak to just one person attending the ceremony.

The first Despacho ceremony I attended including a bay leaf reading:

"There are matted/tangled issues with family and others. You need to <u>untangle</u> that. Take care of the disarray as it happens so it is not growing things. This is about anything in which there is emotional involvement. <u>Not untangling creates emotional chaos.</u>

Be precise. Be practical. Have clear discernment. Take care of your health, lungs, joints, and digestion. Crossroads are coming up. If changing a job or relationship, wait a few months. Bring "order." The old order is not working and is changing. Embrace and adopt the new order."

Place the Quintus around the shell. Bless and pray over the Quintus as you place them. If creating the Despacho in a group, one person may be designated to place all the ingredients. However, it is perfectly all aright if all participants add some of each ingredient. Make a Southern, or equal-armed, Cross of sugar over the flower of Quintus and the shell. The center of the cross meets in the shell. The cross represents community. The Southern Cross represents the Village First, the self, second. In North America, generally the self is placed before the Village. The shell represents the womb, the source from which life emerges. Place a little candy doll in the shell to symbolize yourself emerging. Sprinkle rice around the Quintus to symbolize fertility and enter into a space of inspiration. Sprinkle peanuts to represent the people of the Amazon, the rain forest, the plant people. The rice and peanuts go around the edge of the shell over the Quintus.

Sprinkle lima beans to represent the holy places in the land. The Despacho creates a "Waca," a church of the land. Sprinkle corn next to represent the light, the tears of the sun. Sprinkle tobacco to represent the sacred/secret direct experience for which there is no language. You may also use sage, rosemary, or lavender with the tobacco.

Sprinkle garbanzo beans to represent the Llancas, a patrilineal, seminal right to impregnate the land to be able to maintain a lineage of growth in the land. Add red and white carnations, which track your healed state, your state of well being, and your state of synchronicity with that which is your highest possibility that is meaningful to you.

Add raisins to represent the ancestors and a piece of magnetite for the law of attraction. Add mica (silica) to hold the integrity of your soul and strengthen your psyche. The mica and magnetite also help to anchor the Despacho to the land. Add lavender to call the land spirits. Add sun and moon sequins and silver and gold rods, or little "flutes," to represent the sound in the Andes ("have to hear it, not see it, to believe it"), the voices of the spirits.

Add amaranth seeds (or quinoa) that contain the highest amount of nutrients and vitality. This seed from the Amazon symbolizes opposites that complement the whole. Add llama fat from the chest of a white llama (this one is hard to find) or use buffalo fat to symbolize energy in its finest form, or use a piece of beef fat or butter. Add little figurines of houses, cards, keys, etc., made of metal to represent those things in your life. Sometimes you can find charms that work well for this part. Be sure and remove from the package things like knifes, coffins, locks, etc. that you do not want.

Add two small candles for the light. Little birthday candles work well. You may use any color except black. Add candy figurines for the winged ones, the upper states of consciousness. Add a piece of the "unborn" (a llama fetus in Peru or a piece of jerky in North America) to return to the Mother. Add a starfish to represent the heavens. Add candied stars and fruits to represent fruition, that which you are becoming.

An old dried fig is added to represent the spirit of the mountain, the home of the ancestors. Add a whole round cracker to represent wholeness. Pull a piece of cotton into the shape of a cloud and place it on top to represent the upper realm (this is a good place to recycle the cotton in medicine bottles). On the top of the clouds, add a feather and a strand of rainbow yarn or ribbon to represent the rainbow bridge to fly between the worlds.

Add candy stars to represent the heavens. Add sage for the spirits. Add more flowers to show a healed state. Sprinkle incense on top of all so the offering smells good. Add more stars or sprinkles of many colors around the whole. This is a celebration of life! Decorate the gift with whole flowers. It may look like a cake made of flowers at this point.

Ring a bell over the Despacho and pray over the whole. Then, take a small glass of red wine and a small glass of white wine and, using a flower of the same color, sprinkle a few drops of wine over the whole. Bring the small glasses of wine to the fire and give the red wine to Mother Earth. Toss the white wine up to the mountain spirits when you light your fire.

Wrap your gift. Wrap from the bottom up and from left to right. Tie the Despacho with ribbon <u>without turning the package upside down</u>. Place one more Quintu on top for any forgotten prayers and add the flowers used for the sprinklings, ring the bell again, and pray! The whole now looks like a birthday gift for the land! Underneath are your prayers and visions. In the center is all that represents you, the land, heaven, and Earth. On top is the fruition. The whole is a metaphor of growth and germination.

Now, it is time to take the Despacho to the fire. Fire ceremonies can be created for a variety of purposes, limited only by the extent of your ability to imagine. Healing, honoring the ancestors, walking in Ayni with the Earth, removing past attachments, honoring the dead or dying, are examples of issues you can "take" to the fire. When offering a Despacho, each member of the group may also wish to offer individual gifts and prayers. Each person should clear their Luminous Body and three centers of exchange in the smoke after their gift is given to the fire. Approaching from each direction, up to four people can approach the fire at a time to offer these gifts.

In traditional ceremonies, each person offers her or his own creation, a form of mini-Despacho, created for their personal growth or healing. In healing, there are three important elements:

1. Release,
2. Balance, and
3. Imprint.

Each center of exchange is cleansed, filled, and balanced in the smoke. After each person is done with her or his personal offering, the person's Mesa is circled in the fire seven times, imprinting the Mesa with her or his prayers. Then, each person who wishes to offer healing energy for another person (*i.e.*, a friend, family member or pet) goes again to the fire. Each person's healing path is different. It is not up to us to decide their journey or to do energy work on anyone's behalf without their direct permission. However, it is not always possible to obtain permission. Occasionally, many of us have a strong urge to "do something" for another whether or not that person shares our beliefs. When offering for another person, add the gift of tobacco or sage or flowers to the fire.

However, this time, only the heart center is cleansed and balanced, and our prayers are offered for the best and highest good of the other person or situation. By now, the fire should be a bed of burning coals, and it is time to offer the Despacho to the land.

When the Despacho is placed on a bed of hot coals, elementals, other spirits, and energies of the land, are honored and will come to consume the gift. Make sure the fire is large enough to consume the size of the gift you are offering. Once the coals are hot and not too smoky, create a nest for the Despacho. Gently place the Despacho in the fire with your final prayers. Cover the gift with hot coals. It is respectful to hold the space without being in the way so the spirits can do their thing. In other words, turn your back on the fire while the Despacho burns. Better yet, turn your back and walk slowly away. I place the Despacho and turn my back. I hold the space, thanking the land, breathing in the essence of the ceremony, and all the prayers being released. I wait for Spirit to let me know when to walk away. Sometimes, I will get a distinct push in the middle of my back. Sometimes, it feels as if my shoulder is being tapped. When I get the word from Spirit, I walk away. In a large group, most people get this kind of nudge at the same time. However, all should leave when the first person starts to walk away. The ceremony blesses and awakens the space.

Everything is proportional. It is about generosity. The spirit of the fire will embrace you when you approach with integrity. In healing, in walking into your healed state, you are able to be in Ayni. Spend time in Sacred Space and create your gift for the fire. Gather combustibles from your garden, bless them with your breath and intention, or use them in a Nature Painting. Create a Despacho. Then bring your gift(s) to the fire.

Kutti Despacho:

A Despacho to help you disconnect from the past and move into the future

Kutti Despachos are a very powerful tool of transformation. Whenever someone is stuck, not moving forward, or has been surrounded by negative energies of work or relationship and needs to move forward, a Kutti Despacho ceremony may help. It allows all negative energy from all places in an individual's past or present life to fly away, never to return. This is an involved ceremony and requires quite a lot of time to plan and organize.

Gathering all the needed supplies takes quite a bit of work and time. Kits are often available for purchase. It can be a little difficult to find pieces of snakeskin, and it is not legal for most people to possess hawk and/or condor feathers, but, whatever the feather used, it represents that strong energy. Substitute those feathers from game birds that *are* legal, such as turkey or pheasant, or use goose or duck feathers, if you are not using a kit. Also, it is preferable to use herbs and spices that are locally available. You might want to include basil or rosemary from your own garden, even if using a kit, if you have these or other items, available to you.

The ceremony requires a minimum of two people, one acting as the Shamanic practitioner and one for whom the work is being done. Other people attending are there to witness and hold Sacred Space. The ceremony also takes two to four hours to complete. Fire ceremonies can be held only at noon or dusk, so plan carefully. Kutti Despachos are best done during the day. Your fire should be ready to receive your Kutti and Ayni Despachos at noon. Plan your time accordingly. It is useful to have several people working with the fire while the "Shaman" and "client" create the Despachos.

All participants should begin the morning by clearing self and space, both physically and energetically. Cover a table with a Black Cloth. A large piece of fairly sturdy white paper holds the Despacho. Fold the white paper in thirds both directions and then lay it down on the cloth. A piece of black tissue paper is folded in thirds in each direction so there are nine squares. Lay the black paper on top of the white (it should be a little smaller). The Despacho is created in the center of the black paper and wrapped in the white. Set out all the supplies and materials you need for both the Kutti and Ayni Despachos, as these are created and burned together. Place a sharp knife on either side of the black paper. If you have swords, use them instead. Open Sacred Space. Rattle and chant until you feel ready to begin. Set your intention to clear yourself and your energy body of all negative thoughts and feelings.

Instructions and Supplies for the Kutti Despacho:

- Use one cup of red wine as an offering to Pachamama. After all the Quintus have been created, take the remaining wine and offer it to the Earth with a prayer.

- Use one cup of white wine in the same way as an offering to the Apus, the sacred mountain spirits. When the Quintus are created, take the remaining wine out and toss it into the air with your prayers to the Apus.

- You will create three beautiful Quintus with the most beautiful bay leaves you have, trying to match their sizes.

- You will create 47 additional Quintus and will need lots of broken bay leaves. The ugliest leaves you have available are used to create the Kutti Despacho, with the exception of the three perfect Quintus.

- Write the full name of the client on a Yellow Candle. Take the candle and rub it all over the client's body. Then light the candle, and let it burn throughout the ceremony. Put any remains in the Despacho at the end of the ceremony.

- Light a black candle, and let it burn for the entire ceremony. Put any remains in the Despacho at the end of the ceremony.

- An ugly shell and sacred water are next. Place the shell in the center of the paper and put a few drops of sacred water in it (preferably water from a Pacharina like the ocean or a sacred lake).

- Llama fat—put a piece of llama fat or butter on each Quintu before it is placed in the Despacho.

- Dip each one of three perfect Quintus in red wine and pray over them. Place them in the shell face up. These should be the best and most balanced leaves you can find. The first Quintu you place is for the client. Use his or her full name during the prayer. The second Quintu is to the direction West. This is the energy of the setting sun. It is also the energy of Chocochinchi. The third perfect Quintu is dedicated to the mountains.

Each of the following Quintus are prayed over and then placed in the designated place around the shell. For these Quintus, use the worst bay leaves you can find. Place the leaves face down. The intention here is to release all cords, threads, influences, or obstructions that may be affecting the client in any way that does not serve his/her highest good. This intention is stated in each of the directions with the purpose stated below:

4. North. Family of client. Use full names if you know them.

5. South. Mother and father of client.

6. East. Lover of client.

7. West. Work or profession of client.

8. NW. Spiritual worth/values of client.

9. SE. Friends of client.

10. SW. Business of client.

11. NE. Love relationship of client.

12. NWW. Relationships of client.

13. SEE. Neighbors of client.

14. NNW. Spiritual development and work of client.

15. NNE. Past negatives of client.

16. SWW. Spiritual land and sacred places that have been forgotten.

Next you will add items for protection. These are added to the Despacho in a counter clockwise fashion with the left hand. Pray over each item, and place it in the Despacho on top of the Quintus and around the shell.

- Red chile peppers, the hottest available
- Hot chile powder
- Llama meat, if you have it, or some kind of fat
- Incense (copal, frankincense, or myrrh for protection)
- Feather of turkey or goose (representing Eagle, Hawk, or Condor)
- Fur of deer or guinea pig. Any kind of fur you can find works here.
- Small black flutes
- Snake skin
- Star anise
- Garbanzo beans

- Mustard seeds
- Red clay of the mountains if you have it, or dirt from the client's land
- 2 cocoa leaves (or bay leaves) are waved over the smoke of the yellow candle and prayed over for protection
- Black candle with the alphabet written on it (this is a new candle, not the one burning at the beginning)
- Inkan cross (you can find one in the beading section of most craft stores)
- Stones from the mountains (or stones from the local area to represent the mountains)
- Tools (or items representing everyday tools)
- Black beads
- Protection herbs and seeds—pray over each and place the following around the shell counterclockwise with the left hand for protection (use herbs that are local if that is all that you have)
    o Angelica
    o Basil
    o Caraway
    o Cinnamon
    o Cloves
    o Comfrey
    o Dragon's blood
    o Fennel
    o Garlic
    o Horehound
    o Marjoram
    o Nettle
    o Onion

    o   Rosemary

    o   Palo Santo

    o   Yerba Santa

    o   Peach seeds

    o   Black corn

    o   Small shells

- Rainbow string to encircle all the ingredients
- Fold the Despacho up, right side to left, then top to bottom. This is opposite of how an Ayni Despacho is folded.
- Black and gold string to tie the Despacho up.
- Wooden spears, like BBQ skewers, can be used. Stick them into the tied Despacho.
- Sprinkle white wine on the outside of the Despacho.
- Wash hands with Florida Water

The Shaman then places his/her left hand on the head of the client and with the other hand passes the Despacho over the entire body of the client while praying for protection and clearing. Using two swords, the Shaman then cuts away cords and attachments on the client's body: front, back, sides, and then from hands and feet

The Shaman cleanses the client's body by spritzing the client with Florida Water front and back.

Then, the client holds the yellow candle. The Shaman places his/her right hand on the client's head and prays for the client. The Shaman prays, using the client's full name, for protection and positive energy.

Boil a whole white carnation for a few minutes. When the water has cooled a little, ask the client to take a bath or shower and pour this water all over her or his body.

Next, create an Ayni Despacho to balance all the energies. These are then burned together. When burning the Despachos, create a very hot fire and place both Despachos in when the fire is burning very well. Dowse the fire with olive oil and leave the area as quickly as possible. Indeed, run away as fast as you can as all that old negative energy is released and then re-balanced. Do not look back! You will need to check on the fire in 20 to 30 minutes or so make certain that everything is burning and being combusted. However, you should not go close to the fire unless it looks like there may be a problem. Just make sure it is safely burning. You might need to add more olive oil or Florida Water to get it to burn completely. A Kutti Despacho must be burned. It cannot be buried. The next day, bury anything remaining.

Aya Despacho

Aya Despachos honor the dying, as well as help the recently deceased cross the rainbow bridge. This Despacho honors the soul's journey. For that reason, it can also be modified and created for other joyful transitions like births and weddings. The gift is beautiful and full of joy and memories.

For this special Despacho, you will use seven different colors of paper. Several pieces of tissue paper work well. You are creating a rainbow of colors and layers. Begin with a large piece of black paper. This will be the wrapping for your offering. Think of this Despacho as a present. Fold the paper into thirds one way and then thirds the other way so you have nine squares. Working within the center square, you begin to layer the burnable objects that have been informed with your breath, so the energetic essence of your prayers is within each one.

Offer a drop or two each of red and white wine to both the Earth and to the heavens. Each person attending the ceremony creates a Quintu using three small leaves from your native trees or herbs. If nothing is growing, use bay leaves. Be sure to have enough leaves of similar shapes available. For this Despacho, I like to use leaves of sage, basil, or other herbs or flowers growing in my yard. Quintus are added at several stages of the Despacho's creation.

Red and white carnations honor the Earth and the mountain spirits. Place a red and white carnation petal on top of each Quintu and visualize the snow-covered mountains reaching to the heavens on top of the Earth. Inform each Quintu with your prayers as you work. If doing ceremony with family members, each should be asked to create a Quintu and place all their prayers for their loved one into the Quintu. There their prayers will be transformed in the fire.

Now create the following layers with the colored paper, your prayers and ingredients:

1) Begin with the black paper. This layer represents the Lower World, the unmanifest and potential. Each element added is a symbol of the unmanifest.

i)   Place sugar to represents sweetness and love in the four directions, using breath and intent.

ii) Place your first set of Quintus onto the paper.

iii) Add seeds and animal fat (fuel).

iv) Add representation of the masculine and feminine.

2) Add the red paper to represent the Pachamama. In gratitude, add:

i)   Lots of chocolate. Pachamama loves chocolate;

ii) Candles (not white as they are for the mountains);

iii) Red wine to say thank you to Pachamama (pass it around so that others may sprinkle it over the creation);

iv) Photo of person;

v)   Sprinkles to celebrate life;

vi) Incense;

vii) Herbs, such as sage; and

viii) Seeds, to represent what grows on the Earth.

3) Next, add the green paper representing the present worlds of reality. In gratitude to this level of reality, add:

i)   Animal fat for fuel;

ii) Fruit, raisins, dates to recognize the spirits of our ancestors, our blood lineage;

iii) Alphabet noodles for language, our spoken words;

iv) Garbanzos or peanuts to symbolize all food our Mother provides; our nourishment

v)   Quinoa for sustenance;

vi) Tools, little figures, etc. as aspects of everyday life;

vii) A dollar bill, money for abundance in the next place;

viii) A magnet or grains of magnetite to attract our prayers

ix) Seeds of the Earth; and,

x)   A cinnamon stick, for the spices of the Earth.

4) Add the blue layer of paper to represent the sky, clouds, and sacred mountains. In gratitude, add:

i)   Sugar, for sweetness;

ii) Cotton balls to represent clouds;

iii) Silica, for its magnetic qualities;

iv) White corn for fertility;

v) White beads representing air spirits;

vi) Angels;

vii) White grains like rice or white popcorn, for growth; and

viii) White feathers representing flight.

5) Next, add the purple paper, representing the rainbow layer. This represents the colors of the chakras and the rainbow bridge that may be used by the departed to cross over. In gratitude, add:

i) A shell, the container for the intent of the Despacho;

ii) Inside the shell place a figure that connects the human and the sacred in order to match the departed with his or her cosmic twin;

iii) Multicolored wool or rainbow ribbons to represent the rainbow bridge;

iv) Flowers;

v) A piece of string to surround the Despacho, showing the circle of life;

vi) Confetti to represent joy; and

vii) Incense.

6) Then the gold or yellow paper is added to represent vision, alignment with destiny, and becoming one with the stars. Place the second layer of Quintus here and add:

   i) Copal or any golden incense to carry our dreams;

   ii) Silver and gold leaf for the knowledge of Spirit and of the mystery of the moon;

   iii) Gold and silver flutes for the music in our lives;

   iv) Starfish so all remember "as above, so below;" and

   v) Seeds for continued growth.

7) This last layer of paper is white and covers all the other layers. It is the layer of oneness/nothingness. There is really nothing to do here but honor it with your intention. When you have placed all your items in the Despacho, the corners of the large paper are then folded over the contents so that they all overlap at the center. The Despacho is now a smaller square. The Despacho is tied, without flipping it over so all the prayers are sustained. Add one Quintu to the top for forgotten prayers.

The Aya Despacho is burned for quick transformation within a short time after completion. At the fire, participants may want to share stories and memories; do a reading; or share other prayers for the departed. At this fire, there are no personal offerings or cleansings in the smoke. When the Despacho is placed into the fire, participants do not look toward the flames until after the offering has burnt. This symbolizes non-attachment to the outcome and release of all claims to what was given away. It is also a way of honoring all those who "dine" on the offering and assist the loved one with his or her crossing.

The list of ingredients above is only a suggestion. Items important to the person or animal being helped can be added with the prayers of the people involved in creating this gift. The more you work with Despachos and ceremony, the more creative you can be. Listen to Spirit and know that whatever you do is most certainly "right." Your prayers and intentions carry the energy of the Despacho to the mythic and spiritual levels where they are transformed.

Immediately after I learned the death rites, I was called upon to perform them for several people who had passed and lived quite a distance from me. It was an honor and privilege to perform these rites. I was able to gather a beautiful set of stones to represent the chakras. I used the Young Living essential oil called "Joy" to seal them. Sitting with this process after the unwinding gave me a sense of peace and closure that I had not before experienced with the death of a close friend or family member.

I also used these rites to assist my 15-year-old dog, Angus, to make his transition. He had been my heart dog from the moment we met and had a deep connection that seemed to span lifetimes. As his body became consumed by cancer, and it was plain that his days were short, I decided to do ceremony for him. I gathered all the ingredients I would need, including a beautiful picture of my boy and little dog stickers and buttons to represent his friends. I invited all his old friends, both people and dogs, to a party to create the Despacho. Even though no one else there had ever created such an unusual gift for the land, everyone was willing. Their Quintus were full of good stories and memories and so much love. We cried and laughed and shared stories of the dogs that were all such good friends. When the Despacho was complete, we all went into the yard, and I lit the prepared fire. As I was chanting, my husband appeared. Angus, who had not been up in several days, walked out into the yard and came to each of his friends to say good-bye. It was a beautiful sight to behold. He passed quietly, with the help of his veterinarian, at home the next day.

From "The Enlightened heart: An Anthology of Sacred Poetry" edited by Stephan Mitchell.

I ask all the blessings
I ask them with reverence
Of my Mother the Earth
Of the sky, moon and sun my father.
I am old age, the essence of life.
I am the source of all happiness
All is peaceful, all in beauty
All in harmony, all in Joy.

From the Peacocks:

See our Song
Join and Sway
Colors fill the sky
Our song wakes the day.

Creating Despachos for Other Occasions

Regularly conducting ceremonies to honor the land and to create Ayni is nurturing to the spirit and enhances one's connection to nature and to your land. Helping others cut ties to negativity or to evil forces at work in their lives is very rewarding. Assisting one's loved ones to transition peacefully or to honor their spirit after they have passed is deeply healing and allows the departed spirit to leave in joy. Other major occasions in life are also worthy of ceremony. A change in employment, a birth, a marriage, a good crop, a drought, a tornado or hurricane, and a beautiful spring day may all be honored through the creation of a Despacho.

Ceremony always begins with intent. For whom is the ceremony being designed? For what occasion? How many people will participate in the ceremony? Are they all familiar with the style of the ceremony? Do you have a script to use to encourage people to respect the sacredness of ceremony or to encourage joyful prayer and dancing? The ingredients for a Despacho may be gathered with the intent of the ceremony in mind. Pictures of items representing a special occasion can be added. Items representing a place or business may be included.

After setting a clear and specific intent, gather the ingredients you plan to include. Always think about the three worlds, or the seven chakras, and plan the layers accordingly. Your intention will be carried through all the worlds and all the layers of the chakras as they manifest in the world. Organize the ingredients in the order you will add them to the Despacho.

Go to the area of your fire or the space you will bury your gift. Open Sacred Space. Lay the fire or dig a hole. Open Sacred Space around the area in which you will hold the ceremony and make the Despacho. Let the group be joyful. If you are alone, turn on some music that inspires you. Beat a drum. Dance. Smudge the space. Sometimes ceremonies can last a full day or more.

When in doubt about what to do, create ceremony. When in doubt about how to plan your ceremony, journey and ask Huascar, your spirit guide, or a power animal for help. It is just that simple.

NINE

Working with Others and Energetic Ethics

Once you have completed the process of creating a Healer's Mesa and moved into the collective, you may wish to share this experience with friends and family members. When you have learned to journey safely and are working regularly with a power animal and teacher in the Lower World, you are ready to advance your study. At that point, there are a few gentle energetic practices you can safely do that may also help your friends and family members clear their Luminous Body and begin the process of healing.

When working with others, it is important that you have their permission to do this work. Never work with anyone, human or animal, without permission. If someone is in a coma and permission cannot be granted, you may feel compelled to do the work anyway. If so, do it with the intention that it be accepted only if it is in the best and highest good of "x" and that if "x" rejects the work ask that it go out into the Universe where it can do the most good.

Shamanic work is not a substitute for medical care and should not be offered or considered as such. However, the work is a powerful tool to help people who are ready to do so to release old patterns that no longer serve them and move forward to fulfill their soul's purpose. In that spirit, you can offer help for healing. In this work, it is important to recognize that "healing" and being "cured" are not necessarily the same thing. Someone looking to be cured may not be ready to seek healing. Likewise, a person can move into a healed state without being cured.

Power Animal Retrieval

When a friend is going through a rough patch, it is possible that her or his power animal has abandoned them and she or he needs this help to continue on her or his journey with confidence. It is always nice to have a little help and focus when going through a hard patch like a change in employment or marital status. A power animal retrieval is a nice place to start.

Begin by discussing with your friend the role a power animal can play in helping with problems. Explain how to journey to the Lower World. Power animals can be recognized through hobbies and collections and appear to others as very mainstream. My family, for example, knows that I collect giraffes. They do not know that a very special giraffe, and recently his child, help me with healing work on a regular basis. When I get stuck, I always ask my giraffe friend for advice on where to place my hands or what step to do next. He is a trusted friend and companion, and I am honored by this connection.

The journey to retrieve a power animal for another person is very similar to the one you used to retrieve one for yourself. When you are both ready to start, put a blanket on the floor and lie down on it next to your friend. You should be touching someplace, usually the feet or legs. Cover both your eyes with an eye pillow, towel, or folded bandana as you would for any journey, and enter the Lower World as you usually do. This time your intent is to find a power animal for your friend. As you ask Huascar to enter, ask him to also help you find a power animal for "X." Call out for "X's" power animal. You may see many animals. However, the power animal you are seeking will appear three times. The third time you see that kind of animal, ask specifically: "Are you 'X's' power animal? Are you willing to come back with me to help 'X'?" If you have seen a herd of animals three times, ask for an individual from that herd to come with you.

When an animal answers in the affirmative that it is "X's" power animal and agrees to come with you, wrap your arms around him or her and bring him or her into your heart. Journey to reality, and, as you come back to awareness, blow the essence of your journey, and this new animal, into the heart and crown chakras of your friend. Tell your friend about the animal. Look up information about this animal in books or on-line. Then, your friend should create a dance honoring this new partnership. As Shaman, you can drum while your friend embraces his/her new friend in the dance. When this part is complete, create a fire ceremony or Ayni Despacho to further honor this new connection. Provide some guidelines so your friend can learn the animal's name and they can continue to work together.

Decoupling Fight and Flight

With a healthy energy field and all our chakras working in right relationship with events in our world, it is much easier to think the world a safe and healthy place to be. Most lives are not so simple. Sometimes, things happen that are scary or hurtful, and the energy field is damaged. The chakras hold the hurt and fear. When one is wounded early in life, it may change the world into a very "unsafe" place. The world becomes a hostile world, and anything different or changing is viewed with fear and skepticism. When the world is unsafe, feelings of "fight or flight" are triggered in the body. The fight-or-flight response can get stuck and repeat over and over in the body, especially when it was triggered by trauma. There are people so hurt or frightened at such a young age that they have been in this state for all of their lives.

Decoupling disengages this dynamic in our bodies, and it allows us to relax and begin to engage with the world from a different place. A fully functioning fight-or-flight response is needed to survive this world. The automatic sympathetic nervous system response enables us to run from danger. The adrenals pump adrenaline and cortisone hormones into our system. The heart rate increases, pumping more blood to the extremities.

Originally, we would actually run from the tiger and that released the response from our physical body and Luminous Field. The hormones actually would be used and balance brought back to the system. The parasympathetic nervous system would come back on line, sending nourishment to the life-giving properties of the internal organs allowing ease and rest. The physical body needed to sleep deeply to recharge. But, once the fright was over and the physical body rested, that was it. We moved on with life.

In the modern world, there are lots of unidentified stressors and lots of stressors over which we seem to have little control. There are not very many tigers from whom to flee, but there are many other things that get our hearts racing anxiously just the same. The flight response is initiated, but we are not able to run away so it is never released. Relaxation does not occur, and the body does not recharge. Many people live in a constant state of underlying fear and are not able to relax or sleep restfully. With constant flight or fight engaged, our adrenals get exhausted—they are on overdrive. Cortisol affects our memories and brains. We can get high blood pressure, develop poor digestion, and have nervous systems constantly on edge. Many people are in this state for 20 to 40 years or more. The trigger never leaves the physical or energetic body and becomes super active. Just thinking about a past problem can retrigger the response.

Cleansing the chakras releases what created the original need to take "flight." However, the system can get stuck on "high" even if the stimulus is cleared and no longer there. The Decoupling procedure releases the flight response. The process may need to be repeated two or three times before a new response to the stimulus is created. It may take a week or more for your client to recognize all the effects of the Decoupling. Decoupling is often done in conjunction with an Illumination.

Decoupling:

1. Open your Wiracocha around yourself and around your client.

2. Place your right hand under the heart chakra. Your left hand holds the deepening points at the base of the skull. Connect to the heartbeat of the Earth. The heart is the great drum of the body. Attune your client to that heartbeat. Mentally speak to your client's heart like you would to a child: "It is ok my little one. You can relax, it is safe." Sense the heart coming to rest in your palm over the heart chakra, releasing the tension. The client's breathing will change.

3. Place your left hand under the heart, your right hand under the sacral chakra. Sit in stillness, connecting the heartbeat of the Earth, and attuning the client to that heartbeat. Mentally speak to the client's second chakra, saying: "It is ok my little one. You can relax. It is safe." Sense the second chakra coming into rhythm and balance with the heart.

4. Hold the heartbeat of the Earth for a few moments as the work settles into the client's Luminous Body.

5. Have your client share his or her experience.

6. Close your Wiracocha.

The Spirit Canoe: A Coordinated Lower World Journey to
Restore Personal Power

A "Spirit Canoe" is a form of Shamanic journeying done in a coordinated group setting with the specific intent of restoring power to a single individual. A group of people, adept at journeying, travel to the Lower World and connect with one of their power animals. They form a unified group in the shape of a canoe. The group journeys following the instruction of a fellow journeyer designated to lead. Another journeyer (located in the center of the canoe) works with the person whose power is to be restored (and who is also located in the center of the canoe formation). The journeyer in the center of the boat, acting as "Shaman," restores the client's power through retrieval of an animal. Using the guidelines discussed in Chapter 7, the Shaman identifies, retrieves, and returns with a power animal (either new or missing). The animal is then blown into the person in the center of the boat (into the solar plexus and into the crown chakra). The person in the center of the boat whose animal is retrieved, is then instructed to welcome and get to know the animal by journeying with it, learning about it (including its name), honoring it, etc., as a friend, guardian, and teacher. If successful, such retrieval helps in all facets of life.

Participants form the canoe by sitting on the floor in the shape of a canoe. It is important that all participants be in physical contact in the formation so there is an unbroken line. One of the journeyers will drum throughout the journey. All participants will close their eyes during the journey. The lead journeyer will provide instructions to the group during the journey and may want to write these out before beginning.

When the drumming starts and the signal is given, journeyers will be asked to imagine themselves seated in a large canoe, journeying to and then arriving in the Lower World by paddling (in the journey state, as well as physically paddling) along a river in the tunnel to the other side. The journeyers will be asked to connect with their power animal upon arrival in the Lower World so that these power animals would join in the journey. It is perfectly acceptable to act out the power animal (staying in place and maintaining the canoe formation) and to vocalize the sounds of the power animal to facilitate merging with the animal guide.

KEY: The journeyers who make up the boat also have the job of holding Sacred Space and the integrity of the canoe. So, if *anything* tries to get into the boat, *push it back out with the oar*. Do NOT let anything or anyone into the boat! Not even your power animal!

When the journeyer locating and collecting the power animal for the person whose power is to be recovered has done so, the group will be notified and asked to turn the canoe around and start back. The drummer will then give the signal for the journeyers to thank their power animals for their service and then return to the physical world. Upon return, the journeyer who has collected the power animal will place and blow the power animal into the solar plexus and crown chakras of the person seeking the restoration of power.

That done, the group of journeyers will be debriefed, and the person whose power animal was retrieved will be instructed to work with and get to know the retrieved animal to solidify the bond. Generally, this is done by dancing and becoming one with or truly merging with the new animal as the group drums and rallies its support. The dance reinforces the power of the new relationship and allows the animal to merge with and reside within its new person. After the dance, the person should journey with his/her new animal often, cementing the band of friendship and help. Designating a special space on your altar, or collecting statues or other forms of art work showing your animal, also help to remind one of the new bond and enhance the union to this new source of personal power.

Illumination

The Luminous Field holds everything that has ever happened to an individual. It contains a blueprint of things that have happened and some that did not. The Luminous Body carries blueprints for things like chronic injuries in the same place in the body or similar emotional reactions to things that happen regularly. There may also be blueprints in the DNA (having the same thing as another relative, like high blood pressure, diabetes, or other health issues). The field needs to be cleared so that the body does not hold the things there that no longer serve one well. To clear the Luminous Body, you reach to the eighth chakra, your soul star or individuation point. During the Illumination, the veils between the worlds, both seen and unseen open further. This veil is another protective device for a person's healing. Ask Spirit to open the veil.

Ask Spirit for advice in completing the clearing. When you ask, Spirit responds.

As density builds up in the Luminous Body, so do the themes to which their density relates (this could be a theme of victimization, betrayal, loss, etc.). These themes create density in the field, and, over time, the field can weaken, allowing dis-ease in the body. The goal is for the client to release anything that holds him or her, or keeps him or her, from clear vision. The Shaman's job is to find the original source of the block so it can be released.

When working with others, use your Mesa. Your Kuyas can help you to see more clearly. They can help you on your journey. Have your Mesa present. When working with others, open your Wiracocha over yourself and over your client. With the Wiracocha open, you can see or sense what needs to be done.

As you work with your client, be aware of the different levels of the Luminous Body. There are seven levels, which correspond to the seven major chakras in the body. As density builds, it moves to the physical. Dis-ease develops in the physical. If you clear the field, the healing can come through both the physical and luminous bodies. Travel out of time; see the origin of the wound. Where did it begin?

The Illumination Process:

First, open your Wiracocha over yourself and your client. Then, ask your client to write down some physical things going on in his/her body. Is anything going on emotionally? Is there a lack of something? Ask if there are still some themes (like loss, hopelessness, betrayal, deep sadness, rejection, pain) that need work? Are they "up front" in the field? Have you repeated again something you thought you released or may not have released the first time? You want to look for energetic patterns to release (from either your own or a client's Luminous Body).

Follow up with an interview. "What brings you here? What's going on physically? Emotionally? Is anything happening over and over?" Sometimes people may respond that they have a fear of something and that may give you an idea of the theme. Find out a little about what is going on. Identify the theme or issue that has the most "charge" for your client. If you need to do so, track back and find that memory that was stored in the DNA. You may journey to the Lower World and ask Muki to help you find the root cause of the person's problem, the source of original wounding.

Take your Mesa and clear it with Florida Water. Know that clearing your Mesa also feeds it. Clear it often. Choose a stone from the Mesa. Choose instinctively. Give it to the person and ask her or him to close their eyes and bring up the issue. Bring it up from the belly. Once the issue is up, ask the person to strongly blow that issue into the stone. Repeat twice more. Really get the issue up and into the stone.

Take the stone and hold it in your non-dominant hand. With a pendulum, starting at the root chakra, begin to check the chakras. The lowest chakra discharging, spinning counterclockwise, is holding the issue. That chakra is helping the person work with that issue and her or his physical body may be affected. Work

on the lowest chakra only. When it clears, all the others will
clear, too. If you get that all the chakras are going clockwise
or counterclockwise the person's field may be closed. Ask an
innocuous question (like "when's your birthday?" or "where did
you grow up?") to distract their mind. Recheck.

Once you know which chakra is discharging, open your
Wiracocha over yourself and your client a second time. Rattle in
the field over all the chakras, opening and expanding the field. Use
Florida Water and spritz the field. Move the dense energy out of
the chakras. Backwash the chakra a few times with the rattle (by
moving the rattle counter-clockwise above the chakra and circling
up and out) and then put your stone on the chakra.

Go to the client's head and place your fingers at the base of the
neck. Gently massage and expand those indentations at the base
of the head. This is an important energetic center and a deepening
point. Then, place your fingers on either side of the indentation and
hold gently. Instruct the person to breathe in through the nose, out
through the mouth. Tell the person that the stone is a magnet for
the density around their issue. You can tell the person that the stone
is like a suction cup, clearing the field of all density. You can also
occasionally rattle over the chakra. Hold the head.

Ask the person to go to that fear or loss and tell them to ask
the stone to bring all the density around the issue into it. The
stone brings in the density. The stone is a dense energy magnet.
Sometimes, the body may move, the person may cry, etc. That is
fine. Instruct the person again to breathe in through the nose and
out through the mouth. Bring all the density into the stone so it can

be discharged. Sometimes, you may feel you need to pick up and clear the stone and then replace it. That is fine, too. You can move your fingers out a little, release, and then back to the deepening points. Help the person to deepen. When the chakra is spinning clockwise, help the person to release by encouraging the body to relax deeply. If someone gets really overwhelmed, ask her or him to cross his or her arms over her or his chest. Wait and see if they want to continue.

Work with this process until you sense that the energy has released and the chakra is going clockwise. You may see the body relax, or the person may sigh. You might feel the pulses on the neck relax and beat in rhythm with the heart and the breath. When done, remove the stone. As Shaman, fill the chakra with three scoops of light from your eighth chakra. Rattle around the chakra in a clockwise way. Sit for a while until the person recovers and is ready to get up. Close your Wiracocha. Clear your stone and return it to your Mesa.

Postscript

I have observed that many people attend a retreat or spiritual class, bond with others in the group, and leave feeling renewed and changed. Over the course of the next weeks and months, however, all those good feelings and new energy dissipates, leaving one pretty much as they were, and in need of another nice retreat! Another class is found. Enthusiasm generated and bags packed. Home again all full of new and exciting things to do, and again, it fizzles.

The Shamanic way of walking in the world is no different. Do not feel dejected if your feelings ebb and flow. There is more than one way to get where you need to be. Within these pages, and at workshops that cover this path, you are given a set of tools. These tools can be pulled out, just like the hammer in your kitchen drawer, and used to shore up and enhance almost anything else happening in your life. Remember that there are always options and possibilities to shift that issue to where you need it in the <u>now</u>. Diagnosed with a serious illness? Moving or changing jobs? Getting married? Divorced? Helping a loved one to die? Go to your toolbox for help in adjusting to these new life circumstances.

Your toolbox is large. You can create a Nature Painting, using a Kuya to help your issue transform. Find the chakra holding your issue and clear it. Write out your problem and take it to the fire. Create a Despacho. Choose a candle (of the appropriate color for the day you are doing the work or for the issue on which you are working) and do a clearing of your Luminous Field. Let the candle's flame transform your issue. Shape shift to a new level of awareness. Too close to a problem, or too emotional? Move to Amaru or Apuchin. Having trouble seeing the details? Look at the issue through the eyes of Amaru. Still not clear? Use word deconstruction to move the issue through all three levels of awareness. Then take it all to the fire.

Journey with Muki or Huascar. Ask your totem animals and spirit guides for help and guidance. They are always there waiting to help. No time? Running late? Stop and breathe. The 7-7-7 breath can bring you back to yourself.

Pachamama will be waiting whenever you are ready. Whenever you are ready, that time becomes <u>now</u>. Take a few moments each day to organize your day. Be still. Be present. Rattle your day into being. Dream your life into a state of being that more than fulfills your wildest dreams. Step into the <u>now</u> and be. You are not alone.

APPENDICES

QUECHUAN SELF-PRAYER

To Call on Pachamama and the Apus:

Hampui Pachamama, Santa Tierra Madre, pachamamita—Earth Mother

Yapa Apu Kuna, hatun Ausangate Hampui—mountain beings

Hatun Huaman Lipa, Hampui—Falcon that returns—Apu that protects the rites

Yapa Inka Kuna—luminous ones

Yapa Maiku Kuna—first being to whom God entrusted creation

Yapa Pampamesayoq Kuna—all members of the Pampamesayoq lineage

Yapa Apus Kuna—all members of the Altomesayoq lineage

Yapa Chaska Kuna—star beings

Yanapa waiku chaska chiwaiku, ama hima kakuichu—Let me embody the energy of the stars and creation—let the stars live within me and protect me that this energy of the unmanifest not consume me.

Hampui muchis mamay—mother, feminine side

Hampui muchis papay—father, masculine side

Come to me Pachamama, come Mother of the Mountains, little
mother, come to me.
Mountain Beings come to me.
To the Falcon that returns, to the Mountain Spirits who protect
these rites, come to me.
Luminous ones, Angels to whom God entrusted creation, come to me.
Guardians of the Earth, come to me.
Star Beings come to me.
Let me embody the energy of the stars and creation.
Let the stars live within me and protect me, so this energy will not
consume me.
Creation energy of the feminine, come to me.
Creation energy of the masculine, come to me.
Fill me Mother. Guide my steps. Show me your ways.

Hampui sounds like HUM-PWIE

SONG TO THE APUS

Apu Ausangate Humpuyai Hampui, Bandeira, Bandeira

Apu Salcantay Humpuyai Hampui, Bandeira, Bandeira

Apu Huanakauri Humpuyai Hampui, Bandeira, Bandeira

Apu Sacsayhuaman Humpuyai Hampui, Bandeira, Bandeira

Apu Machu Picchu Humpuyai Hampui, Bandeira, Bandeira

Apu Huayna Picchu Humpuyai Hampui, Bandeira, Bandeira

Apu Huaman Lipa Humpuyai Hampui, Bandeira, Bandeira

Apu Huaca Wilka Humpuyai Hampui, Bandeira, Bandeira

Apu Illimani Humpuyai Hampui, Bandeira, Bandeira

Apu Pacha Tucson Humpuyai Hampui, Bandeira, Bandeira

Apu Everest Humpuyai Hampui, Bandeira, Bandeira

Apu Shasta Humpuyai Hampui, Bandeira, Bandeira

Apu Hood Humpuyai Hampui, Bandeira, Bandeira

Apu Rainier Humpuyai Hampui, Bandeira, Bandeira

This song is chanted to welcome and call the Apus, and it may also be sung to establish and strengthen one's connection to the Apus, the mountain spirits, the Apu Khuna.

Pronunciations: Humpuyai sounds like HUM PWEE
Hampui sounds like HUM PWIE
Bandeira sounds like Ban DAY ra

GLOSSARY

Apus (heights noted when known) and other Sacred Sites of Qosqo (Cusco)

Ausangate (Vilcanota range, 20,790 ft.)

Salcantay (Vilcanota range, 20, 575 ft.)

Veronica (Urabamba range, 18,865 ft.)

Pachatusan, "Fulcrum of the Universe"

San Boleyn

Santa Warmi

Killa Wasi

Pancha Kollyu

Mama Simuna

Huaca Wilka

Machu Picchu (7,677 ft.)

Huayna Picchu (the mountain you see behind Machu Picchu in most pictures)

Manuel Pinto

Yanantin (notched peak that can be seen from Ollantaytambo. The two notches represent the bringing together of differences, *e.g.,* masculine and feminine principles, 14,718 ft.)

Sacred Sites in North America and Elsewhere

Everest (Himalayas, 29,029 ft.)

Mt. Rainier (Cascade range in North America, 14,411 ft.)

Mt. Shasta (Cascade range in North America, 14,179 ft.)

Qosqo (Cusco) Rivers

Huatanay, West side of Qosqo

Sappphi

Tica Tica

Tullumayo, "spine" of Puma-shape; east of Qosqo

Urubamba, "Sacred Valley" of the Incas; runs past Machu Picchu
   to the Amazon

Vilcanota, Southern section of Urubamba

Basic Quechua Vocabulary

Note: The Quechuan language is just beginning to be placed
into a written form. Over time, it has merged with Spanish, and
the pronunciation is similar to Spanish. My linguistic ability is
not such that a guide to pronunciation may be provided. This
list was given to me at my first workshop. Sadly, the source was
not noted. When searching the internet for spelling variations,
I found the following useful websites: http://www.inkawisdom.
org/andeanTraditions/spirituality/concepts.html, and http://www.
incaglossary.org/h.html.

Aclla, chosen woman, virgin of the sun, etc.

Allinyachiy, cure; heal

Amaru, Snake, Inca symbol of knowledge, lore

Amaut'a, teacher

Anka, black-bodied eagle

Apu, spirit of the mountain; protector

Auki, old man; spirit

Aya, death

Ayllu, kinship group; Royal clans of Qosqo

Ayni, reciprocity, offering back to creation

Ch'uya songo, of pure heart

Chaska, Inka messenger from Heaven to Earth

Chiqchi, hail

Chullpa, round burial tower

Coca, coca tree; daughter of Pacha Mama introduced by American
    John Styth Pemberton in 1886

Cusi, energy body, aura

Cuzco (Qosqo), navel; holy city of the Incas

Qosqo, navel energy center (chakra)

Despacho, offering

Hamp'ard, altar; table used in rituals

Hanaqpacha, upper world

Hatun laika, master shaman; sorcerer

Huaman, hawk

Hucha, heavy energy

Hujupacha, the lower world (interior world)

Husca, sacred site, shrine

Illapa, lightening

Inti, sun

Inti Taita, Father Sun (similar to Christ)

Intiwatana, Hitching Post of the Sun

Kallanka, great hall (common in Inca architecture)

Kaq'lla, ray of lightening

Katachillay, the Southern Cross

Kay Pacha, this world, the middle world

Kechua (Quechua), Peruvian Indian tribe; their language

Kenti, hummingbird

Killa, moon

Koyllor, star

Kuntur, condor

Kuta k'intu, a ritual offering of select coca leaves

Kuya, amulet in form of animal or god

Laika, sorcerer

Lika, non-Christian tradition

Llankay, belly

Machay, cave

Machu, old, ancient

Mama Cocha, Mother Ocean

Mama Quilla, Mother Moon (identical with Virgin Mary)

Mama Sara, Corn Goddess

Mastay, order

Mayu, river

Mijuy, to eat

Much'ana, altar; place of worship

Mullumarka, Monastery; place of the holy stones; love; chest

Naupa, old, ancient

Neustas, spirits of lakes, springs or lagoons/ponds

Pacha, cosmos, era

Pacha Kamaq, Creator God

Pachamama, Mother Earth, female cosmic energy on this planet (similar to Virgin Mary)

Pako, healer

Pampa, flat place

Pana, right wide

Picchu, peak

Pucara, fort

Puna, high Andean grassland, above tree line

Q'ero, last of the Inca tribes

Q'uyas, power rocks in the Andes

Qolgi, silver color

Qori, gold color

Quilla, hill

Quinoa, Andean high altitude grain

Quintu, three coca leaves used in fortune telling, or Despachos. They represent the literal, symbolic, and mythic; the three worlds (Lower, Middle, and Upper); and flow, connectivity, and vision (Amaru, Chocochinchi, and Apuchin).

Quipu, knotted-string recording device

Quya hampeq, "he who cures with stones"

Raqua, ruins

Riti, snow

Runa, being; person

Salka, wild, undomesticated (puma vs. cat)

Sachamama, spirit of South; great serpent of Lake Yarinachocha

Sami, spirit of plants

Sonquo, heart

Tambo, lodging house; temporary storage house
Teqse muyu, energy of the Universe
Toqo, to gather in, in Despacho, bringing leaves into the center
Tumi, ritual knife

Ukuku, bear man

Wanka, eagle
Warmi, female
Wayra, wind
Wilka, Sacred
Wiracocha, Creator God, Luminous Field, Luminous Body

Yachay, knowledge, mind; head
Yankay, work

Predominant Inkas:

Manko Qhapaq, First Inka; founder of Qosqo
Pachacuteq, Founder of Inka Empire
Huayna Capac, Last Inca over united empire
Manco Inka, leader of rebellion against Spanish from Vilcabamba
Tupac Amaru, last Inka

Three Levels of the Hierarchy of Mountains

Ayllu Apu, Apu of small community
Llaqta Apu, Apu of village; also the priest who works with this energy
Suyo Apu, Apu of region

Three Aspects of Relationship in the Andes

Tinquy, seeing another for the first time and investigate (like a wolf
    would)
Tupay, level of confrontation
Take, conjunction, communion; inner loving state

Three Levels of Andean Cosmos

Pacha (Andean cosmos):
    Hujupacha, interior world/Lower World
    Kaypacha, this world/surface/work/Middle World
    Hanaqpacha, Upper World/superior/atmosphere

Levels of Initiation into Andean Knowledge

First are the Pampamesayoq, "Guardians of the Earth," who
perform the rituals of the land, and work with energies of the
Earth, and Spirits of the Earth.

Next are the Altomesayoq, a more advanced Shaman, who also has
a connection with supernatural beings, primarily in the Apus.

Third are the Curaq akulleq, "great man," "elder"; literally, "the great masticator of coca leaves." To chew coca means to meditate, so *Curaq akulleq* is a great meditator and visionary, an awakened one.

There are two levels above these, but they may not be named.

Resources

Books

There are dozens of interesting and well-written books about Shamanic practices from a variety of cultures and perspectives on the bookshelves today. Each offers a glimpse into a new way of visioning the world and many provide exercises and practices for enhancing one's skill in journeying. Some of my favorites are:

Andrews, Lynn. *Medicine Woman*. San Francisco, CA: Harper and Row, 1981.

Andrews, Ted. *Animal Speak*. St. Paul, MN: Llewellyn Publications, 2004.

Harner, Michael. *The Way of the Shaman*. New York, NY: Harper and Row, 1980, 1990.

Ingerman, Sandra and Wesselman, Hank. *Awakening to the Spirit World*. Boulder, CO: Sounds True, 2010.

Ingerman, Sandra. *Shamanic Journeying*. Boulder, CO: Sounds True, 2004.

Madden, Kristin. *The Book of Shamanic Healing*. St. Paul, MN: Llewellyn Publications, 2002.

Matthews, Caitlin. *Singing the Soul Back Home.* Boston, MA: Connections Books, Ltd., 1993.

Sams, Jamie. *The Sacred Path Workbook*. New York, NY: HarperCollins Publishers, 1991.

Villoldo, Alberto. *Shaman, Healer, Sage.* New York, NY: Harmony Books, 2008.

Wilcox, Joan Parisi. *Ayahuasca: The Visionary and Healing Powers of the Vine of the Soul.* Rochester, VT: Park St. Press, 2003.

_____. *Masters of the Living Energy*. Rochester, VT: Inner Traditions, 1999.

<u>Supplies</u>

Additional information about Despacho kits and specialty kits made in the USA: http://www.prayerbundles.com

Despacho kits, drums, rattles, Florida Water, pendulums, and other items to make your own Despachos can often be found at: http://ebay.com

Despacho supplies, kits, Mesa cloths, rattles, drums, books, and CDs: http://www.ShamansMarket.com and http://www.Shamansstore.com

For courses and additional resources: the Foundation for Shamanic Studies, founded by Michael Harner: http://ShamanicStudies.com.

Pendulums and information about dowsing and divination: http://www.diviningmind.com.

Tarot Card Decks

I have an addiction to divination decks. From "angel" cards to "totem animal" cards to "tarot" cards, I collect card decks. Every time I went to a workshop, I brought along my newest deck. Often, by the time others in the class tried to order a copy for themselves, the deck would be out of print, and the cost of a used copy prohibitive. Amazon.com and Ebay.com are good sources for used card decks. Be sure to carefully clear both your new, and especially your used, cards. My favorites and the ones I use most often are:

Carr-Gomm, Philip and Stephanie. *The Druid Animal Oracle.* New York, NY: Simon and Schuster, Inc., 1994.

Ryan, Mark and Matthews, John. *The Wildwood Tarot.* New York, NY: Sturling Ethos, 2011.

Winter, Gayan S. and Dose, Jo. *Vision Quest Tarot.* CH-8212 Neuhausen, Switzerland. http://tarotworld.com.

INDEX

M

N